Inheritance

Inheritance

A Memoir of Genealogy, Paternity, and Love

DANI SHAPIRO

Alfred A. Knopf
NEW YORK
2019

THIS IS A BORZOI BOOK
PUBLISHED BY ALFRED A. KNOPF

Copyright © 2019 by Dani Shapiro

Library of Congress Cataloging-in-Publication Data

Names: Shapiro, Dani, author.
Title: Inheritance : a memoir of genealogy, paternity, and love /
Dani Shapiro.
Description: First edition. | New York : Alfred A. Knopf, 2019.
Identifiers: LCCN 2018024082 (print) | LCCN 2018050939 (ebook) |
ISBN 9781524732721 (ebook) | ISBN 9781524732714 (hardcover)
Subjects: LCSH: Shapiro, Dani. | Women novelists, American—Biography. |
Novelists, American—20th century—Biography. | Jewish women—United
States—Biography. | BISAC: BIOGRAPHY & AUTOBIOGRAPHY / Literary.
| BIOGRAPHY & AUTOBIOGRAPHY / Cultural Heritage. | BIOGRAPHY &
AUTOBIOGRAPHY / Personal Memoirs.
Classification: LCC PS3569.H3387 (ebook) | LCC PS3569.H3387 Z46 2019
(print) | DDC 818/.5403 [B]—dc23
LC record available at https://lccn.loc.gov/2018024082

Jacket photograph by Diana Weymar
Jacket design by Carol Devine Carson

Manufactured in the United States of America
First Edition

This book is for my father.

Author's Note

This is a work of nonfiction. In some cases, names and identifying details have been changed in order to respect and protect the privacy of others, and to keep a promise I made from the very start.

I shall never get you put together entirely,
Pieced, glued, and properly jointed.

—Sylvia Plath, "The Colossus"

If you want to keep a secret,
you must also hide it from yourself.

—George Orwell, *1984*

Part One

I

When I was a girl I would sneak down the hall late at night once my parents were asleep. I would lock myself in the bathroom, climb onto the Formica counter, and get as close as possible to the mirror until I was nose to nose with my own reflection. This wasn't an exercise in the simple self-absorption of childhood. The stakes felt high. Who knows how long I kneeled there, staring into my own eyes. I was looking for something I couldn't possibly have articulated—but I always knew it when I saw it. If I waited long enough, my face would begin to morph. I was eight, ten, thirteen. Cheeks, eyes, chin, and forehead—my features softened and shape-shifted until finally I was able to see another face, a different face, what seemed to me a *truer* face just beneath my own.

Now it is early morning and I'm in a small hotel bathroom three thousand miles from home. I'm fifty-four years old, and it's a long time since I was that girl. But here I am again, staring and staring at my reflection. A stranger stares back at me.

The coordinates: I'm in San Francisco—Japantown, to be precise—just off a long flight. The facts: I'm a woman, a wife, a mother, a writer, a teacher. I'm a daughter. I blink. The stranger in the mirror blinks too. A daughter. Over the course of a single day and night, the familiar has vanished. *Familiar: belonging to a family.* On the other side of the thin wall I hear my husband crack open a newspaper. The floor seems to sway. Or perhaps it's my body trembling. I don't know what a nervous breakdown would feel like, but I wonder if I'm having one. I trace my fingers across the planes of my cheekbones, down my neck, across my clavicle, as if to be certain I still exist. I'm hit by a wave of dizziness and grip the bathroom counter. In the weeks and months to come, I will become well acquainted with this sensation. It will come over me on street corners and curbs, in airports, train stations. I'll take it as a sign to slow down. Take a breath. Feel the fact of my own body. *You're still you,* I tell myself, again and again and again.

2

Twenty-four hours earlier, I was in my home office trying to get organized for a trip to the West Coast when I heard Michael's feet pounding up the stairs. It was ten-thirty in the evening, and we had to leave before dawn to get to the Hartford airport for an early flight. I had made a packing list. I'm a list maker, and there were a million things to do. *Bras. Panties. Jeans skirt. Striped top. Sweater/jacket? (Check weather in SF.)* I was good at reading the sound of my husband's footsteps. These sounded urgent, though I couldn't tell whether they were good urgent or bad urgent. Whatever it was, we didn't have time for it. *Skin stuff. Brush/comb. Headphones.* He burst through my office door, open laptop in hand.

"Susie sent her results," he said.

Susie was my much-older half sister, my father's daughter from an early marriage. We weren't close, and hadn't spoken in a couple of years, but I had recently written to ask if she had ever done genetic testing. It was the kind of thing I had never even considered, but I had recalled Susie once mentioning that she wanted to know if she was at risk for any hereditary diseases. A New York City psychoanalyst, she had always been on the cutting edge of all things medical. My email had reached her at the TED conference in Banff. She had written back right away that she had indeed done genetic testing and would look to see if she had her results with her on her computer.

Our father had died in a car accident many years earlier, when I was twenty-three, and Susie thirty-eight. Through him, we were part of a large Orthodox Jewish clan. It was a family history I was proud of and I loved. Our grandfather had been a founder of Lincoln Square Synagogue, one of the country's most respected Orthodox institutions. Our uncle had been president of the Orthodox Union. Our grandparents had been pillars of the observant Jewish community both in America and in Israel. Though as a grown woman I was not remotely religious, I had a powerful, nearly romantic sense of my family and its past.

The previous winter, Michael had become curious about his own origins. He knew far less about the generations preceding him than I did about mine. His mother had Alzheimer's and recently had fallen and broken her hip. The combination of her injury and memory loss had precipitated a steep and rapid decline. His father was frail but mentally sharp. Michael's sudden interest in genealogy was surprising to me, but I understood it. He was hoping to learn more about his ancestral roots while his dad was still around. Perhaps he'd even enlarge his sense of family by connecting to third or fourth cousins.

Do you want to do it too? he might have asked. *I'm sending away for a kit. It's only like a hundred bucks.* Though I no longer remember the exact moment, it is in fact the small, the undramatic, the banal—the *yeah, sure* that could just as easily have been a shrug and a *no thanks.*

The kits arrived and sat on our kitchen counter for days, perhaps weeks, unopened. They became part of the scenery, like the books and magazines that pile up until we cart them off to our local library. We made coffee in the mornings, poured juice, scrambled eggs. We ate dinner at the kitchen table. We fed the dog, wrote notes and grocery shopping lists on the blackboard. We sorted mail, took out the recycling. All the while the kits remained sealed in their green and white boxes decorated with a whimsical line drawing of a three-leaf clover. ANCESTRY: THE DNA TEST THAT TELLS A MORE COMPLETE STORY OF YOU.

Finally one night, Michael opened the two packages and handed me a small plastic vial.

"Spit," he said.

I felt vaguely ridiculous and undignified as I bent over the vial. Why was I even doing this? I idly wondered if my results would be affected by the lamb chops I had just eaten, or the glass of wine, or residue from my lipstick. Once I had reached the line demarking the proper amount of saliva, I went back to clearing the dinner dishes. Michael wrapped a label around each of our vials and placed them in the packaging sent by Ancestry.com.

Two months passed, and I gave little thought to my DNA test. I was deep into revisions of my new book. Our son had just begun looking at colleges. Michael was working on a film project. I had all but forgotten about it until one day an email containing my results appeared. We were puzzled by some of the findings. I say *puzzled*—a gentle word—because this is how it felt to me. According to Ancestry, my DNA was 52 percent Eastern European Ashkenazi. The rest was a smattering of French, Irish, English, and German. Odd, but I had nothing to compare it with. I wasn't disturbed. I wasn't confused, even though that percentage seemed very low considering that all my ancestors were Jews from Eastern Europe. I put the results aside and figured there must be a reasonable explanation tied up in migrations and conflicts many generations before me. Such was my certainty that I knew exactly where I came from.

In a cabinet beneath our television, I keep several copies of a documentary about prewar shtetl life in Poland, called *Image Before My Eyes*. The film includes archival footage taken by my grandfather during a 1931 visit to Horodok, the family village. By then the owner of a successful fabric mill, he brought my great-grandfather with him. The film is all the more powerful for the present-day viewer's knowledge of what will soon befall the men with their double beards, the women in modest black, the children crowding the American visitors. Someone—my grandfather?—holds the shaky camera as the doomed villagers dance around him in a widening circle. Then we cut to a quieter moment: in grainy black and white, my grandfather and great-grandfather pray at the grave of my great-great-grandfather. I can almost make out the cadence of their voices—voices I have never heard but that are the music of my bones—as they recite the Mourner's Kaddish. My grandfather wipes tears from his eyes.

In the year before my son's bar mitzvah, I played him that part of the documentary. *Do you see?* I paused on the image of the rough old stone carved in Hebrew. *This is where we come from. That's the spot where your great-great-great-grandfather is buried.* It felt urgently important to me, to make Jacob aware of his ancestral lineage, the patch of earth from which he sprang, the source of a spirit passed down, a connection. Of course, that tombstone would have been plowed under just a few years later. But in that moment—my people captured for all time—I was linking them to my own boy, and him to them. He hadn't known my father, but at least I was able to give Jacob something formative that I myself had grown up with: a sense of grounding in coming from this family. He is the only child of an only child, but this—this was a vast and abundant part of his heritage that could never be taken away from him. We watched as the men on the screen swayed back and forth in a familiar rhythm, a dance I have known all my life.

So that 52 percent breakdown was just kind of weird, that's all, as bland and innocuous as those sealed green and white boxes had been. I thought I'd clear it up by comparing my DNA results with Susie's. Now, on the eve of our trip to the West Coast, Michael was sitting next to me on the small, tapestry-covered chaise in the corner of my office. I felt his leg pressed against mine as, side by side, we looked down at his laptop screen. Later he will tell me he already knew what I couldn't allow myself even to begin to consider. On the wall directly behind us hung a black-and-white portrait of my paternal grandmother, her hair parted in the center, pulled back tightly, her gaze direct and serene.

Comparing Kit M440247 and A765211:

Largest segment = 14.9 cM
Total of segments > 7cM = 29.6 cM
Estimated number of generations to MRCA = 4.5

653629 SNP's used for this comparison
Comparison took 0.04538 seconds.

"What does it mean?" My voice sounded strange to my own ears.

"You're not sisters."

"Not half sisters?"

"No kind of sisters."

"How do you know?"

Michael traced the line estimating the number of generations to our most recent common ancestor.

"Here."

The numbers, symbols, unfamiliar terms on the screen were a language I didn't understand. It had taken 0.04538 seconds—a fraction of a second—to upend my life. There would now forever be a *before*. The innocence of a packing list. The preparation for a simple trip. The portrait of my grandmother in its gilded frame. My mind began to spin with calculations. If Susie was not my half sister—*no kind of sister*—it could mean only one of two things: either my father was not her father or my father was not my father.

3

A sepia photograph of my father as a little boy hangs just out-side our living room, where I pass it dozens of times a day. He poses in a herringbone coat and bowler hat, white kneesocks and shoes, playfully holding a cane. His eyes are round, his smile impish. He was the oldest son born into a family obsessed with recording itself—a family conscious of its own legacy. Grandparents, great-uncles, great-aunts, even distant cousins from the old country are scattered throughout my house. But it is the portrait of my father that is my favorite. *Who is that?* friends will ask. *My dad,* I will answer. He has been dead more than half my life and still the feeling is the same: a warm, quiet pride, a sense of connection, of tethering, of belonging.

The portraits and sepia photographs can be traced to the Eastern Europe of my forebears. My ninety-three-year-old aunt Shirley—my father's younger sister—has been the family archivist. Years ago, she entrusted Michael and me with the task of digitizing the contents of a massive leather-bound fam-ily album. Jagged-edged photographs traced an evolution from the dusty shtetl to prosperous turn-of-the-century America. Michael took each one from the album and created an online version to share with the grandchildren, great-grandchildren, and great-great-grandchildren, now numbering in the hundreds. *There's Grammy and Grampy about to set sail for Europe.* My grandparents were regal and glamorous next to a trolley piled high with their steamer trunks. *There's Rabbi Soloveitchik and Uncle Moe with Lyndon Johnson. There's Moe with John Kennedy.* Men in yarmulkes next to presidents, their faces proud and lit with purpose.

These ancestors are the foundation upon which I have built my life. I have dreamt of them, wrestled with them, longed for them. I have tried to understand them. In my writing, they have been my territory—my obsession, you might even say. They are the tangled roots—thick, rich, and dark—that bind me to the turning earth. During younger years when I was lost—particularly after my dad's death—I used them as my inner compass. I would ask what to do, which way to turn. I would listen intently, and hear them answer. I don't mean this metaphysically—not exactly. I'm not sure what I believe about where we go when we die, but I can say with certainty that I've felt the presence of this long-gone crowd whenever I've sought them. My dad, in particular, would come to me in an electric tingle running the length of my body. I was convinced that my father was able to reach me through time and space because of the thousands of people who connected us.

L'dor vador. These Hebrew words, one of most fundamental tenets of Judaism, translate into *from generation to generation.* I am the tenth and youngest grandchild of Joseph Shapiro, self-made industrialist, philanthropist, a leader of modern Orthodoxy: chairman of the presidium of the Mesifta Tifereth Jerusalem, treasurer of Torah Umesorah, vice president of the Lubavitcher Yeshiva, member of the national board of the Union of Orthodox Jewish Congregations. I am the tenth and youngest grandchild of Beatrice Shapiro, his beautiful, gracious wife, who was admired and emulated by religious women of her generation the world over. I am the daughter of their oldest son, Paul. Everything I am, everything I know to be true, begins with these facts.

I woke up one morning and life was as I had always known it to be. There were certain things I thought I could count on. I looked at my hand, for example, and I knew it was my hand. My foot was my foot. My face, my face. My history, my history. After all, it's impossible to know the future, but we can be reasonably sure about the past. By the time I went to bed that night, my entire history—the life I had lived—had crumbled beneath me, like the buried ruins of an ancient forgotten city.

A Zen meditation made popular by the twentieth-century Indian sage Ramana Maharshi goes like this: the student begins by asking and answering the question Who am I?

I am a woman. I am a mother. I am a wife. I am a writer. I am a daughter. I am a granddaughter. I am a niece. I am a cousin. I am, I am, I am.

The idea is that eventually, the sense of *I am* will dissolve. Once we're past all our many labels and notions of what makes us who we think we are, we will discover that there is no *I*—no *us*. This will lead us to a greater understanding of the true nature of impermanence. The exercise is meant to go on long past the most obvious pillars of our identity, the ones beyond question—until we run out of all the ways we think of ourselves. But what does it mean when the *I am* breaks down at the very beginning of the list?

4

There are many varieties of shock. This is something you don't know until you've experienced a few of them. I've been on the other end of a phone call hearing the news that my parents were in a car crash and both might not live. I've sat in a doctor's office being told that my baby boy had a rare and often fatal disease. I have felt the slam, the blade, the breathless falling—a physical sense of being shoved backward into an abyss. But this was something altogether different. An air of unreality settled like a cloak around me. I was stupid, disbelieving. The air became thick sludge. Nothing computed.

"Maybe they got it wrong."

Michael just looked at me.

"Switched vials? Mislabeled the results?"

It was the thinnest of threads, but it was all I had. Human error. It seemed possible, in that moment, that all of this would turn out to be a big mistake, something that would become a crazy story I'd tell someday, after I'd recovered from this needless distress.

"Let me see if I can get someone on the phone," Michael said.

He paused in the door to my office.

"You okay?"

"I'm fine." My voice was reedy, stretched taut.

Alone in my office, I went back to ordinary things with a vengeance. I unplugged my phone charger from the wall and wrapped the wires neatly around it. I packed up my travel-size toiletries and checked them off the list. I looked up the San Francisco weather and folded an extra sweater into my bag.

Estimated number of generations to MRCA = 4.5

Susie and I were four and a half generations away from a most recent common ancestor. At first this didn't seem like a lot of generations, but within a single ethnic group like Eastern European Ashkenazi Jews, by four and a half generations, just about everyone has an ancestor in common. Close relatives—parents, uncles, aunts, first, second, even third and fourth cousins—are pinpointed by DNA testing sites with a degree of precision. If two people share a father, the results would be resoundingly clear.

Susie and I were not related.

Somewhere within me, in a place as dangerous and electric as a live wire, I knew what this meant, if it was true. *If it was true* being something that I would repeat to myself again and again. *If it was true* being something that I might always cling to, in a disbelieving, childlike way, part of the thick sludge.

If it was true that Susie and I were not half sisters, my father was not my father.

That he was Susie's father was without question. She looked like him. She had his eyes, and the shape of his face. She even sounded a bit like him, her cadences those of a born-and-bred, yeshiva-educated New Yorker. I, on the other hand, looked nothing like my father or like anyone in his family. I was pale-skinned, very blond, blue-eyed. All my life, I'd fielded and deflected comments about not looking Jewish, but I had no reason to question my biological connection to my dad. He was my *dad*. But now—in a minefield of doubt—there was no doubt in my mind about Susie's paternity. Only about mine.

The more chaotic my thoughts became, the more precise my actions, as if carefully folded T-shirts and jeans might fix everything. I could hear Michael's voice downstairs. Had he gotten someone on the phone at this hour? Where was Ancestry.com even located? I imagined a massive warehouse full of thousands of plastic vials.

I was trying to think it all through, but with a mind blunted as if by a sledgehammer blow. Vladimir Nabokov, in *Speak, Memory,* ponders the question of how to examine a deluded mind when one's only resource is a deluded mind. I picked my way through the little I knew. First of all, that business about being 52 percent Eastern European Ashkenazi in the DNA analysis. That was ridiculous. Of course I was entirely Jewish—my parents were both Jewish. I had been raised Orthodox. I mean, I was *very* Jewish. I spoke fluent Hebrew until I was in high school. I had always countered the litany of questions about my ethnicity with a recital of my impeccable family history. That plastic vial must have been accidentally switched with that of some half-Jewish person, who was at this very moment confused about her own DNA.

My results had also listed a first cousin who was unfamiliar to me. There he was, a blue icon like one that might be found on the door to a men's room, identified only by his initials. This—Michael will later tell me—set off loud, clanging warning bells for him.

But not for me. Obviously I knew all my first cousins. This only reinforced my certainty that there must be some mistake. I ran through the facts of my own identity again and again as if memorizing a poem, or factors of an equation.

By the time Michael came back upstairs, it was nearly midnight. We were leaving for the airport in four hours. I was freezing. He wrapped his arms around me, but not before I saw the look on his face. I registered that I had never seen him look at me that way before. Not when my mother died. Not when our boy was sick. I would describe it as something bordering on pity. It wasn't so much my future that was being irrevocably altered by this discovery—it was my past. Michael had already known this, of course, well before he looked up the toll-free number on Ancestry's website. He had known when he first saw the surprising breakdown of my ethnicity. When a cousin who was a stranger had appeared along with my results like an emissary from some foreign world.

"It's not a mistake," he said softly.

In the ensuing weeks, every person I tell about this night will say a version of the same thing: *Must be a mix-up. It can't be true.* They will say it protectively. Indignantly. They will say it out of kindness. And they will be wrong. Millions of people have had their DNA tested by Ancestry.com, and no such mistake has ever been made.

5

In the immediate aftermath of my discovery, there was one incident—one story—that crystallized in my mind. It was 1988. I was twenty-five years old, and my father had been dead exactly two years. My mother had been badly injured in the car accident that killed my father, and I had spent the previous two years taking care of her. At the same time, I was in graduate school at Sarah Lawrence and I was writing my first novel as if my life depended on it—which, in a way, it did. Writing was my way of trying to give shape to my sorrow. I was alternately numb and filled with searing pain. These seemed my only two states of being. I cut off all my hair, broke up with my boyfriend, quit smoking, quit drinking. All my free time was devoted to reading the poems of Adrienne Rich. I wondered if maybe I was a lesbian. I was a stranger to myself, adrift in the world.

I didn't want my mother to spend the second anniversary of my dad's death alone. I invited her to come with me to school, where some of the graduate students were giving readings. I picked her up at her apartment on West End Avenue and we drove the half hour north together. I didn't have much to say to my mother. I never really had. Our life as mother and daughter had been fraught and contentious, devoid of the easy love I felt for my father. As a child, I'd had the fantasy—a form of hope, now a staggering irony—that she wasn't actually my mother. The silence between us was less companionable than tense and awkward. But we had entered strange new territory since the accident. She had recovered from her injuries far beyond her doctor's expectations. Still, she was frail and walked with a cane. Her face had been smashed to bits, but now it was reassembled, her nose slightly askew, one eye a different shape from the other. As she often reminded me, I was all she had.

Before the reading, the students and faculty gathered for a reception in the living room of the house on campus where each of us would soon read from our manuscripts. It was at this reception that I introduced my mother to one of my classmates named Rachel.

"Rachel, where are you from?" my mother asked.

"Philadelphia," Rachel replied.

"Oh, my daughter was conceived in Philadelphia."

Smooth, without missing a beat.

In twenty-five years, I had never heard this. I pictured a hotel, a romantic weekend getaway. But my mother had already moved on to extol the virtues of the City of Brotherly Love.

"What do you mean, I was conceived in Philadelphia?" I asked.

"Oh, you don't want to know," my mother replied. "It's not a pretty story."

That night—after the earnest readings, the Styrofoam cups of herbal tea, paper plates piled with cookies—I drove my mother down the Saw Mill River Parkway in the winter darkness. Two years earlier, with my mother in critical condition in a New Jersey hospital, I had buried my father in the Shapiro family plot in Bensonhurst, Brooklyn. It had been my first funeral. My father's sister, brother, all my cousins, even Susie seemed to know exactly what to do. The stark service was conducted entirely in Hebrew. One of my cousins, a rabbi, led the service. The rituals of mourning were foreign to me—though I had been raised Orthodox, there were striations of Orthodoxy—and at my own father's funeral I felt like an interloper, out of place amidst my family. *Here's where you walk,* one of my cousins guided me. *Here's a shovel,* another one said. *Now it's time to wash your hands.*

"Mom?"

"Yes, dear?"

"Mom, you can't just say something like that about my conception. You need to tell me what you meant."

Both our eyes were trained straight ahead. The car a confessional, a vault.

"There was a doctor—an institute—in Philadelphia," my mother said. "Your father and I were having trouble conceiving."

She stopped there. We were twenty minutes from her apartment.

"He had slow sperm," she added. And then, after another beat: "I'd had several miscarriages. And I was in my late thirties by then."

"So what happened?"

"I would go to Philadelphia—this was a world-famous institute—and they would monitor exactly where I was in my cycle. Then, when it was time, I'd call your father on the floor of the New York Stock Exchange and he would race down so we could do the procedure."

"What procedure?"

"Artificial insemination."

If I hadn't been driving, I would have closed my eyes. You want the story of your conception to be at the very least corporeal. A man and a woman, limbs entwined. Sperm swimming to egg. Not the sterile clinic I suddenly envisioned, a test tube, a medical version of a turkey baster. Not my father alone in a room with pornography and a Dixie cup.

"I told you," my mother said. "Not a pretty story."

What sharpened my senses that night to such a degree that I would be able to retrieve the conversation in its entirety, thirty years later? At the time, I found the whole thing odd, slightly discomfiting, but of little consequence. Really, what difference did it make how I had been conceived? I was here. Who cared how my father's sperm got to my mother's egg?

Now the details are so clear to me, as if contained in a time capsule: the Hudson River in the darkness; the lights strung across the George Washington Bridge; the even timbre of my mother's voice; the high plane of her cheekbone. Her long-fingered hands clasped in her lap. *Institute. World-famous. Philadelphia.*

6

Bradley Airport near Hartford is a place I know well. A frequent traveler, I have my routine. First stop after going through security is always a small futuristic-looking glass cylinder where for two bucks you can place your eyeglasses inside for a power wash. With satisfyingly clean glasses, my typical pattern is to then proceed to the newsstand to stock up on trashy magazines. After, if time allows, I stop at Lavazza for a mediocre cappuccino to drink at the gate. I find the familiar routine comforting when I travel. It cuts through the usual disorientation I tend to feel when leaving home.

But my standard travel anxieties, which had not been insignificant, were, I now realized, nothing compared to this. I walked unsteadily through the wide halls of the airport like a convalescent. Michael stayed close to me as we passed a wall of projected images—part of an interactive ad campaign for Travelers insurance—depicting a series of red umbrellas made of roses that broke apart into hundreds of petals as each person passed by. People of every shape and size disrupted the umbrellas, causing the petals to scatter in different ways. Children were especially taken with the images. They stopped, jumped up and down, windmilled their arms. *Tohu va'vohu.*

The Hebrew words—from the second sentence of Genesis—
arose in me the way the Hebrew language tended to: like bits
of sediment shaken loose from some subterranean place. *Tohu
va'vohu* meant chaos. The world upside down. No—the world
before it was the world. My body felt strange and weightless.
Was I even here? Maybe I didn't exist. My whole life had been
a dream I dreamt up. As we passed the red umbrellas, I looked
to be sure that my shape registered.

We reached the gate forty-five minutes before boarding.
Michael had his computer open on his lap and was typing
search terms into Google, looking up fertility clinics in Philadelphia that had existed in the early 1960s. His background as
a journalist made this kind of research second nature to him.
It took only a few minutes to zero in on the place it had to be.

"The Farris Institute for Parenthood," he said. "On the
campus of Penn."

Institute, my mother had said. Not *clinic.* Not *hospital.*

A few swift keystrokes and we were reading up on Dr.
Edmond Farris, a trailblazer—*world famous,* my mother had
said—in the field of infertility and artificial insemination.
Another detail my mother had mentioned that night came
back to me. The famous doctor had pioneered a method to
pinpoint when a woman was ovulating. *I'd call your father . . .
and he would race.*

All around us, the airport hummed with travelers going
places. Flights were departing for Atlanta, Detroit, Miami,
Chicago. A tired-looking flight attendant walked past, drag-
ging her small bag behind her. The sun had just begun to rise,
glowing orange over the tarmac. The words blurred together:
sterility, infertility, insemination. And then another couple of
words connected with the Farris Institute for Parenthood:

sperm donor. The term seemed to be sharper than all the rest. *Sperm donor.* I looked up from Michael's screen and all I saw were men: young men, old men, very old men. Men holding babies. Fat men wearing baseball caps. Men in tank tops and track pants. Men in button-downs and cardigans. If my father wasn't my father, who was my father? If my father wasn't my father, who was I?

That February night nearly thirty years ago, after dropping my mother off at her apartment, I went home and called Susie.

"Did you know anything about Dad and Irene having fertility problems?"

"That sounds familiar. I was a teenager, but I knew something was up."

I told Susie what my mother had said. Philadelphia, the institute, the famous doctor, the slow sperm, the urgency, her biological clock tick-tick-ticking, our father's mad dash from New York so they could make a baby.

Susie paused. "And she told you it was definitely Dad's sperm that was used?"

My hand tightened around the phone. My stomach clenched as it often did around my half sister.

"Of course it was Dad's sperm!"

"You might want to look into it," she said. "They used to mix sperm in those days."

Mix sperm. Once you hear a phrase like that you never forget it. Two words that crash against each other, like a nonsensical Mad Libs fill-in-the-blank. Susie said it the way she said most things—in a practiced, seemingly casual way. But beneath it was a current of something alive. She was telling me that I should look into the possibility that we were not sisters. That our father was hers—not mine. My psychoanalyst half sister was expressing a very deep and perhaps not wholly conscious wish: she would have preferred that I had not been born.

I remember my own anger and bitter humor. Analyze *that,* I said to friends. But I did bring it up to my mother the next time we were together. Here is where my memory becomes hazy. We might have been walking the streets of the Upper West Side. She walked a lot in those days to strengthen her legs.

"Mom, I heard something—going back to what you told me about what happened in Philadelphia—"

My mother was unreadable to me, not only in that moment but in every moment. She never let her true self be seen. Her dark eyes often quivered disconcertingly, and when she smiled it was a careful smile—as if smiling was something she practiced in private.

"I heard that sometimes they would mix the sperm . . . ?"

I may not remember whether we were on Broadway or West End or Riverside Drive, but I am clear on one thing: there was no ripple, no tensing, no quick blink. Not a glimmer of surprise or distress crossed my mother's face. She exhibited no confusion at the bizarre phrase.

"Do you think," she responded, "that your father would ever have agreed to that? It would have meant he wouldn't have known if his child was Jewish."

My father's life had been shaped by the rules of observant Judaism. He was a black-and-white thinker. Good, bad, right, wrong. He was also a person who was clearheaded and interested in the truth. Mixing his sperm with those of *any* stranger would have been unthinkable. But a non-Jewish stranger would have been impossible—I was sure of that. His religion was the deepest and most abiding part of his identity—and Judaism wasn't only a religion, it was an ethnicity. His child would have been other. Set apart from the very lineage he came from.

"You knew your father," my mother went on. In my memory, she is looking directly at me. "Can you imagine such a thing?"

7

Throughout history, great philosophical minds have grappled with the nature of identity. What makes a person a person? What combination of memory, history, imagination, experience, subjectivity, genetic substance, and that ineffable thing called the soul makes us who we are? Is who we are the same as who we believe ourselves to be? Philosophers, who love nothing more than to argue with one another, do seem to agree that a continued, uninterrupted sense of self, "the indivisible thing which I call myself," is necessarily implied in a consciousness of our own identity. "The identity of a person is a perfect identity: wherever it is real it admits of no degrees; and it is impossible that a person should be in part the same, and in part different; because a person . . . is not divisible into parts." This, from early nineteenth-century philosopher Thomas Reid.

It might have happened that I discovered the truth of my paternity at a moment when I would be staying—as I often do—at home. I might have sat silent for days on end, in my leather chair in my library, surrounded by the thousands of books that make up at least a portion of my consciousness, books that have taught me how to think, how to live. I might have taken my dogs for long, slow walks. I might have treated myself like a postoperative patient, a person who has been carved up and stitched together. With our son on the other side of the country in a summer film program, the house would have been quiet. In late June, the peonies planted along the back of our house had begun to bloom.

Instead, we boarded a flight to Minneapolis. You can't get from Hartford to San Francisco directly, at least not on Delta, which is where we have our miles. And so I settled into seat 12A, by the window. I pulled my magazines out of my bag and stuffed them into the seat pocket in front of me. A Bachelorette was in the midst of a breakup. A Kardashian was in trouble. I leaned my head against Michael's shoulder. I didn't know how to be, what to do next. I saw my dad's face—not as it was when he was at his happiest but as it appeared in the days after my parents' accident: gray, his eyes vacant, mouth slack. It seemed the essence of him, the spirit of him, was already gone. He died of his injuries shortly after. And then another image: I'm a young woman meeting my father for lunch on Wall Street. The trading floor doors swing open and out he comes: beaming, alive. He wears a tan jacket, the uniform of all the traders; his head is round and bald. The glasses he always wore are nearly rimless, just a glint of gold at the temples. He smiles the hard-earned smile of a wounded man who lives for pockets of joy and is still able to feel them. He is at his most vital in two places: here, where he works, and in synagogue, where he prays. He wraps me in a bear hug as the crowd mills around us.

I squeezed my eyes shut against hot tears. This felt like a second death. I was losing him all over again. I had become divisible. *In part the same. In part different.* A fundamental law of identity—my very sense of self—broken open.

Something that never occurred to me as I flew across the

country, though it would have been reasonable to contemplate: that my mother might have had an affair. But I just didn't go there—I didn't need to. Pieces to an enormous puzzle, the puzzle of my life, in fact, began to click into place with such speed and efficiency that it seemed no other explanation was possible.

The flight attendants made their way down the aisle with the beverage cart. They offered pretzels, granola bars, salted peanuts. The two prior times in my life I had experienced shock and terror—my parents' accident and Jacob's illness—it seemed an impossible affront that people were going about their daily business and that in fact no one's life had changed but mine and those of people I loved. Here I was again. Except a parent's death, shivering over a child—these were common experiences. You could say *my father died* or *my baby's sick* to just about anybody, and they would respond with compassion and understanding. But how about: *I just found out that my dad wasn't my biological father and that apparently I come from an anonymous sperm donor.* I glanced over at Michael's open computer screen. He booted up Gogo Wi-Fi as soon as we reached ten thousand feet and was on my Ancestry.com page, staring at the small blue human-shaped icon, identified only by the initials A.T. My first cousin. A male. Blue for boys.

What next? I couldn't imagine what might come next. I am a spinner of narratives, a teller of tales. I have spent my life attempting to make meaning out of random events, to shape stories out of an accretion of senseless, chaotic detail. As a writer and a teacher of writing, this is what I do. *What if,* I might begin to suggest to a student. *How about . . . ?* But I had been dealing within the confines of a known world. I am not a fantasist. I have never been drawn to mysteries of the whodunit variety, or to sci-fi. Magic realism interests me, but there are limits to my suspension of disbelief. What never fail to draw me in, however, are secrets. Secrets within families. Secrets we keep out of shame, or self-protectiveness, or denial. Secrets and their corrosive power. Secrets we keep from one another in the name of love.

Out my window, the sky was a vivid blue, streaked with clouds. Below, the fields of Wisconsin appeared in orderly rectangles— the opposite of *tohu va'vohu*. Evidence of coherence.

"What do you think the profile of a sperm donor would have been, in the early 1960s?" I asked Michael.

"In Philadelphia," he said, eyes still trained on his computer screen, the blue icon.

"On the campus of Penn."

What was I asking? Even as I posed the question, the words sounded absurd. The sheer vastness of possibility—any man of a certain age could be my biological father—slammed into a lifetime of singularity and conviction. I wasn't my father's daughter. The thought knifed through me, sharper each time I touched it.

"Doctors often donated sperm," Michael said. "And medical students."

Was my biological father a medical student? It was nothing more than a working theory, but one that felt right to both of us. What did *right* even mean? How and where did this shared idea come from? I had never paid any attention to the history of reproductive medicine or artificial insemination.

Hell, I hadn't even watched *Masters of Sex,* though I'd heard it was pretty good. If I didn't come from my father, who did I come from?

"A medical student," I said aloud.

Michael nodded.

"Yeah. A med student at the University of Pennsylvania."

8

The father I knew had always been sad. He wasn't so much a depressive by nature as he was a kindhearted, cheerful person who had been beaten down by life. He had married young—a marriage arranged between two prominent Orthodox families—and that relationship quickly turned unhappy. When Susie was six years old, his first wife left while he was away on a business trip. The story I've been told is that he came home to their empty apartment to find nothing but his clothes hanging in the closet. Divorce was virtually unheard of in the tight-knit community that made up my father's world in the early 1950s. Devastated, he fought for the closest thing to shared custody that existed in those days: he had Susie every Wednesday night and on alternate weekends. A short while into his life as a single father, he fell in love with a young woman named Dorothy. Dorothy was twenty-six when they met—an alluring, incandescent creature with bright eyes and an easy smile, and in the few photographs I've seen of the two of them together, my father's face is soft, unguarded, and full of joy.

They set a wedding date and began to dream of their shared future. But my father had unknowingly become a player in a tragedy. Dorothy had been diagnosed with non-Hodgkin's lymphoma—a death sentence back then—and her family had kept her condition secret from her. My father discovered the truth a few days before their wedding and, against rabbinic advice, telling no one except his best friend and his sister, moved forward with the plan to marry. Dorothy was—many of those who knew them together have told me—the love of his life. She died six months later.

I didn't know about Dorothy when I was growing up. I didn't know to what to attribute my father's unhappiness. Evenings, he slumped in his easy chair watching television. He became sedentary and fat—one of many sources of conflict between my parents—and his belly strained over the top of his trousers. When I was thirteen, his chronic back pain became so extreme that he underwent spinal fusion surgery. He never fully recovered, and he numbed himself with painkillers and sedatives for the rest of his life.

It wasn't until I was a grown woman, a writer—when I had reached the age my father had been when he had been divorced, then widowed—that I became obsessed with knowing more of what had happened. I was convinced that the loss of Dorothy must be the primary locus of my father's pain. And so I wrote an article for *The New Yorker* and painstakingly assembled the crushing details of the brief life he and Dorothy had shared. It felt to me, in the months it took to write that piece, that I was gluing my father back together. This is what I did, what I had always done from the time I first put pen to paper. *Tikkun olam*. I was trying to repair my broken father. To make him whole.

Perhaps—it occurs to me as I write these words—I am attempting to reassemble my father once more.

.   .   .

My father met my mother in the aftermath of Dorothy's death. He had moved into an apartment on East Ninth Street in New York City, and my mother lived on the same block. She was vivacious, intrepid, an advertising executive recently divorced herself. The first time they encountered each other—on *Shabbos*—she was carrying a hammer and on her way to install bookcases in her own new apartment. *He should have known,* my mother would later say. She wasn't from his world. She was Jewish, but not religious. Otherwise she wouldn't have been building bookcases on *Shabbos*. But after months of dating, dazzled by my father and his exceptional family, she agreed to become Orthodox when they married, and to raise their children in an observant home. My father must have been certain that my mother was his last, best chance.

It took my parents five years to have a child. Five years punctuated by miscarriages, and trip after trip to Philadelphia. Five years in which my mother was approaching forty. In the years my parents were trying and failing to have a baby, my father's younger brother and his wife had four children. His younger sister already had four children. One of the most important mitzvahs according to Jewish law: *pru u'rvu*. Be fruitful and multiply.

I thought I understood my father's sorrow. I had written deeply on the subject, not only in *The New Yorker* but also in several of my books. Finally I came to accept that I had learned all I could learn. That he had been unhappy was without question. But at least I had been able to build a monument to him, a stack of stories, essays, memoirs, novels that I wrote in his honor—my own, secular form of *kaddish*. I knew all about his tyrannical, exacting father; his capricious first wife; the loss of his great love; the bitterness of his marriage to my mother.

But there had been something more—something I could never quite fathom. An invisible live wire stretched between my parents and me. Touch it, and we all might go up in smoke. I knew this, too, though I couldn't have articulated it. I had turned away from fiction, toward memoir, as if a trail of words might lead me there. All the while, I wondered: Why did it matter so much? After all, my parents were long dead. I had survived them. I had built a life. I had a family of my own. Whatever their secrets, they were now buried, lost to history. My latest book was the first of my memoirs that had nothing to do with my parents.

It turns out that it is possible to live an entire life—even an examined life, to the degree that I had relentlessly examined mine—and still not know the truth of oneself. In the end, it wasn't words but numbers I stared at disbelievingly on a computer screen that smashed down the door and flooded every corner, every crevasse, with a blinding light: *Comparing Kit M440247 and A765211.*

All my life I had known there was a secret.

What I hadn't known: the secret was me.

Part Two

9

A classic children's book I used to read Jacob when he was small is titled *Are You My Mother?* In it, a baby bird goes off in search of his mother after he falls from his nest. Since he doesn't know what his mother looks like, his mother could be anyone or anything. "Are you my mother?" he asks a kitten, a hen, a dog, a cow. "Are you my mother?" he asks a plane, a steam shovel. The reader roots for the baby bird, of course, as he perches on the nose of a bored dog. "Are you my mother?" But beneath the most obvious reasons we hope for the baby bird to find his mother is an even more profound one. Unless he finds his mother, he will not know who or what he is.

We had a two-hour layover in Minneapolis—another airport I know well. I left Michael to his breakfast and found a quiet spot at a gate across from the restaurant. I had scribbled down a very brief list of everyone I could think of—friends of my parents, elderly relatives, anyone at all who might still be alive, and could possibly know something, anything, about what happened in a fertility clinic in Philadelphia fifty-four years earlier. There were so few people left. My dad's ninety-three-year-old sister, Shirley, was one, but I couldn't possibly call her. If my father wasn't my father, then she wasn't my aunt.

The thought made me tremble, and I lowered myself into a plastic chair bolted to the floor. Grandparents, aunts, uncles, cousins floated away from me like dozens of life rafts. There was only one person I could think of to call: my mother's best friend, who, if still living, would now be in her early nineties. My mother had had very few close friends. Her friendships tended to end in hurt feelings and recriminations. Yet Charlotte, whom she had known since they were college sorority sisters, had remained. I remembered her as kind, sensible, loyal—a temperament that nicely offset my mother's penchant for drama.

I tried to steady myself before dialing Charlotte. I hated the phone in the best of circumstances, preferring email: an introverted writer's refuge. Would Charlotte tell me that everyone had always known I wasn't my father's child? I hadn't known the truth of my own being, and that was nearly unendurable—but if I discovered that my identity was an open secret, withheld only from me, how would I survive it? As the phone rang, my heart raced. Maybe she was dead. Maybe she was senile. Maybe she would confirm my worst fears. In which case I would be left with the terrible awareness that my two dead parents had hidden my very identity from me. I heard my mother's voice: *You knew your father. Can you imagine such a thing?*

My last conversation with Charlotte had been fifteen years earlier, when my mother was on her deathbed. Now, after a few stilted pleasantries—she was alive and lucid—I began to stutter out the reason for my call. This was the first but far from the last time I would have to tell the story to an old person, a very old person, knowing that it might be painful and challenging. How old was too old for a surprise? How old was too old to blow up the past, rather than keep it intact?

"Charl? Did you know that my parents had fertility issues?" I waded in slowly.

"I did. Your mother had quite a few miscarriages."

"Were you aware that they went to a doctor in Philadelphia?"

"Yes. There were many trips to Philadelphia," Charlotte responded. "Your mother desperately wanted a child."

"So you knew that I was conceived by artificial insemination."

"Yes, dear. I knew that. Yes."

There was nothing to do but come out and say it.

"Charl, I've just found out that my father wasn't my biological father," I said.

A second passed, maybe two. I pictured her sitting at the kitchen table in her small New Jersey condo, a mug of coffee by her side. It was still morning, even though Michael and I had already flown halfway across the country. *Please, please, please,* I found myself praying. But for what? And to whom?

"What are you saying?" Her voice shook. "That's impossible."

Impossible. Suddenly I was able to take a deeper breath. She hadn't known.

"Did my mother ever say anything? Anything at all that might have even hinted at—"

"Your mother would have told me," Charlotte said. "She told me everything."

I went on to explain the genetic testing, and the stark fact that I was not related to Susie, along with the mystifying appearance of A.T., a first cousin.

"There must have been a mistake. Maybe they switched the test tubes," she said.

As unseemly as it felt to be telling this to a nonagenarian,
I described what I knew thus far about the practice of mixing
sperm. I was now the conveyor of information, rather than the
recipient. Each word was an effort. All the while, I kept an eye
on Michael, who had gathered his belongings and was making
his way over to the gate where I sat—the wrong gate, it turned
out, unless we were planning to go to Kansas City.

"Oh, Dani. Well, I'm absolutely sure of one thing," Charlotte finally said before we got off the phone. "Your father is
still your father."

It had been eleven, maybe twelve hours since Michael sat next
to me in my office, a sequence of numbers unlocking the combination to a me I hadn't known. In those hours I had felt sorrow, despair, alienation, numbness, shock, confusion—mostly
confusion. And also something else: I was on the hunt. A fact-
finding mission had taken me over, keeping the deeper res-
ervoir of feelings at bay. *Your father is still your father*. It was a
loving thing to say, meant to console, but I didn't know what
it could possibly mean, that my father was still my father. I
was at the beginning of a journey, one that I would walk alone,
step by treacherous step. It felt like a truism, a cliché, a salve. I
loved my father with all my heart and had devoted much of my
life to him. But—in purely clinical terms—he wasn't my father.
There was someone out there—some anonymous man, possibly alive, probably dead, maybe a sperm donor who had once
been a medical student at the University of Pennsylvania—who
technically, biologically, was my father. A point of fact.

Michael and I stepped onto the moving walkway. Still,
quiet, pensive, we glided through the airport. People, people

everywhere. Fellow travelers. An elderly couple moved in the opposite direction. A white-haired man, mid-eighties, wearing a raincoat. I smiled at him and looked swiftly away. Fifty-four was definitely not too old for a surprise. At fifty-four, with any luck, I had a few decades left to live. Would I ever know about that somebody else? Would I ever again feel that my father was my father? Would it always matter? Lines from a Delmore Schwartz poem come to mind: "What am I now that I was then? / May memory restore again and again / The smallest color of the smallest day; / Time is the school in which we learn, / Time is the fire in which we burn."

10

I tell my students, who are concerned with the question of betrayal, that when it comes to memoir, there is no such thing as absolute truth—only the truth that is singularly their own. I say this not to release them from responsibility but to illuminate the subjectivity of our inner lives. One person's experience is not another's. If five people in a family were to write the story of that family, we would end up with five very different stories. These are truths of a sort—the truth of adhering to what one remembers. Then there are facts, which are by their nature documentable. The weather on a particular day can be ascertained. As can the date of the explosion. Perhaps there is a photograph of the dress she was wearing. And so forth. But the intentions of your father? The inner life of your mother? At these we can only hazard our best guess.

Students sometimes tell me that they're waiting for someone to die before they feel they can write their story. They say this sheepishly, guiltily. As if, in some way, they're wishing for that person to expire, already, so they can get on with the business of writing about them. I try to liberate my students from these tortured thoughts by telling them that they may as well just start now, because it can be more difficult to write about the dead than to write about the living. The dead can't fight back. The dead have no voice. They can't say: *But that isn't how it was. You're getting it wrong*. They can't say: *But I loved you so*. They can't say: *I had no idea*.

And so each day when I sit down to write I am wrestling not only with my dead parents but with a dearth of documentable facts. A friend offers to set me up with a world-famous medium the FBI frequently uses as a resource in solving complex cases. "She'll be able to tell you what your father knew," she says. But I can't call the medium, at least not now—not only because I'm skeptical but because I need to arrive at my own beliefs about myself and my parents and the world we inhabited. I need to understand who I was to them, and who they were to me. In the absence of the empirical, I am left with a feeling central to my childhood: all my life I had the sense that something was amiss. I was different, an outsider. My family didn't form a coherent whole. My parents and I lived in a breakable world. I had been deeply, mutely certain that there was something very wrong with *me*, that for all this I was to blame.

Thirty-five thousand feet in the air, between Minneapolis and San Francisco, that mute certainty began to fall away as if I were a molting animal. There *had* been something amiss. We *didn't* add up. And not because I wasn't my father's child but because I—and possibly one or both of my parents—had never known.

II

⁓

The Uber driver who picked us up at the airport in San Francisco in a hulking black Humvee was a six-foot-tall blonde who looked like she'd just walked off a movie set. This only added to the surreality of the moment. San Francisco—though I've passed through on business many times—is not a city I know well. Nor does Michael. Through the tinted windows I caught glimpses of the bay as we hit stop-and-go traffic on the 101. There was construction everywhere I looked, massive cranes dangling high above building sites. We crept along past streets at once familiar and strange, known to me more from literature than from direct experience. Mission, Van Ness, Geary.

I had taken a break from the Internet during the flight from Minneapolis, and now the emails were pouring in, among them a possible jacket design for my new book. It was a beautiful design—very close, in fact, to what ended up as the final cover—a black-and-white photo of Michael and me on our wedding day. But I hated the florid, curlicued type. I noticed that this was possible—my being able to hate the type on a book jacket—something that seemed like a vestige from a previous life.

"It looks like calligraphy on a wedding invitation," I said to Michael.

Our Uber driver, who had been chatty the whole way into the city, was asking about our trip.

"Business or pleasure?"

"A little of both."

"Staying in town long?"

"Just a couple of days, and then on to L.A. Our son is in a film program at UCLA for high school students."

As I would discover in the coming months, I was capable of functioning as if on one side of a split screen. Our driver overheard our conversation about the jacket and asked to see it. As she drove, I handed her my phone. One eye on the road, she agreed that it looked like a wedding invitation. As we reached our hotel in Japantown, my sense of disorientation only grew. We were speaking of normal things. Where to have dinner? I needed to call my editor to talk through the jacket design. But the thick sludge was everywhere. I now understand it as shock: the sense of my own body as foreign, delicate, fractured, and the world at once hostile and implacable in its anonymity.

Our room was spacious and spare, the late afternoon light filtered through windows covered with shoji screens that, when slid open, revealed the low buildings of Japantown. From that particular vantage point, we could have been in any city— Tel Aviv, Berlin. The pagoda a block away wasn't visible from our room. Later, the next day, I would walk past the pagoda to a shopping center filled with sushi joints and tea shops, and spend an hour in a stationery store buying index cards. My instinct was to begin to write everything down—every random thought, even just single words—as a record of a time I might not be able to clearly remember. At some point I will wonder what I meant by *Huxley's Island,* or *"Filius nullius—son of nobody."* Like a drunk in a blackout, I will try to reconstruct what happened and when. From another index card: *Bessel van der Kolk: "The nature of trauma is that you have no recollection of it as a story."*

I unpacked our suitcases quickly, efficiently, with the same military precision with which I had packed the night before. I made a dinner reservation at a bistro a short taxi ride away. It was as if well-folded clothing and the prospect of a candlelit dinner could stave off the rumble of a distant avalanche. I couldn't afford to be quiet or still. I had to keep moving, to outpace whatever might come next.

When I checked my phone, I saw an email from Susie. I had written her at some point over the course of the day. *I don't know how to tell you this but we're not half sisters.* It hadn't been a hard note to write, and I didn't think she'd find it a hard note to read. It didn't disturb me in the least that Susie was not my half sister, nor would it disturb her. This is how we had always referred to one another—half sisters—though I had noticed that in more cohesive families, stepsiblings, half siblings often didn't differentiate themselves but considered themselves siblings, period. Not Susie and me. That *half* was always there. And now it wasn't.

As a girl, I had looked up to Susie. She had written a book—her doctoral dissertation—on schizophrenia, which I didn't understand but that sounded important. She was smart, and worldly. She lived in the West Village, in NYU housing, which seemed like the epitome of adult life to me, a New Jersey kid with inchoate aspirations. Susie tried to be kind to me—and there were a few years there when I was a teenager and we actually got along. Our shared enemy: my mother. Susie hated my mother, and by the time I was fourteen, fifteen years old, I did too. Susie would use words to describe my mother that both terrified and secretly thrilled me: *Narcissistic personality disorder. Borderline.*

I put on lipstick. Changed out of my airplane clothes. Spoke with my editor in New York about the type on the book jacket. I was struggling mightily to stay on the safe side of the split screen. Then I opened Susie's response to my email:

Wow. This must be so difficult for you. Especially since dad and Irene aren't here to process this with you. Could Irene have been trying to tell you in that crazy moment? Let's meet up the next time you're in town or Hamptons.

What it felt like: a sharp, overpowering aloneness. Susie's casual tone only increased my sense of being adrift in the world. I was my mother's daughter. *Narcissistic personality disorder. Borderline.* I had read dozens of books over the years ranging from complex psychoanalytic tomes to straight-up self-help as I tried to navigate the difficulties of being my mother's daughter. But my single best defense had always been that I was my father's daughter. I was *more* my father's daughter. I had somehow convinced myself that I was *only* my father's daughter.

Now—as Michael and I headed to dinner in that vertiginous, magical city, houses and buildings perched in jagged rows on steep inclines—I felt cut loose from everything I had ever understood about myself. The wind kicked up, and my eyes began to tear. How could I survive this new knowledge that I was made up of my mother and a stranger?

12

The following morning, long before I opened my eyes, I heard Michael on the other side of our hotel room, the rapid clicking of laptop keys. Dawn light filtered through the shoji screens, red against my pulsing lids. I ached with grief, but this grief was not the sharp, suffocating grief that accompanies a recent death. It was a field of grief, a sea of it. There were no edges. The night before, a friend had sent me a passage from *Moby-Dick,* a description of a ship in a gale, a caution against the attempt to sail back to land: "In the port is safety, comfort, hearthstone, supper, warm blankets, friends, all that's kind to our mortalities. But in that gale, the port, the land, is the ship's direst jeopardy." Before I fell asleep I read it again and again, as if trying to interpret a spiritual text. I was in a gale. My mind was wild, grasping, seeking solid ground. But there was no solid ground. I kept my eyes closed, trying to orient myself. *You're in San Francisco. Japantown. Your husband is here. It's Thursday, June 30.* One phrase of Melville's had remained with me overnight: "the lashed sea's landlessness."

The sound of Michael at the keyboard was comforting. I was sure he was chasing down leads. I smelled coffee. Michael had spent many years in Africa, investigating warlords and third world dictators, and had written a book that exposed the underside of foreign aid. Dogged research was second nature to him. The work often began with a hunch—and hunches often led to dead ends. Only sometimes they didn't. Sometimes they led straight to indisputable facts. As long as I could hear the sound of Michael typing, it felt as if something was happening.

"You up?"

"Yeah."

Slowly I opened my eyes. The room was dim, Michael silhouetted against the shoji screens. A couple of Starbucks paper cups were next to him on a small table. He had gone to sleep obsessed with my mystery first cousin, A.T. Often, on Ancestry.com, family trees and the pages associated with them are administered by a separate person, and in A.T.'s case, there was an actual name attached to his page: Thomas Bethany. Michael had been digging and digging into all sorts of people named Thomas Bethany, the one identifiable link to A.T., and had come up with nothing but dead ends. There were death records for several men named Thomas Bethany; there was a Thomas Bethany who was a middle school soccer star from Rhode Island. Down the road, Michael will tell me that he found a Thomas Bethany who was a huge supporter of presidential candidate Donald Trump.

Michael brought me one of the coffees, and I propped myself up in bed. Bed was where I wanted to stay. Bed would continue to be a place from which I would try to navigate my ship in the gale.

"It's not Thomas Bethany," he said. "It's Bethany Thomas."

I tried to clear my head. I looked up at Michael. He was wired, hopped up on coffee. I had a feeling he'd been up for hours. Besides, we were still on East Coast time. I grabbed my own laptop from the bedside table and opened it to my page on Ancestry.com. There he was again, whoever he was; the small blue person-shaped icon. He looked so harmless, really, like a cartoon figure.

"Why?"

"A.T.," Michael said. "T."

"I don't get it."

"People tend to do this—administer these things—for their relatives. *T.* Like *Thomas.* Maybe A.T. is the husband, brother, father, whatever, of someone named Bethany Thomas."

I was having a hard time computing. A.T. B.T.—who were these people to me? They were as abstract and surreal as the fractions and decimals representing genetic code.

"Have you gotten anywhere?"

"Not yet. But I'm pretty sure I'm right. I think we should get some help with this. What do you think about calling Jennifer Mendelsohn?"

Jennifer Mendelsohn is a journalist based in Baltimore. We hardly knew her. In fact, I don't think either of us had ever met her. We were friendly with her brother, the writer Daniel Mendelsohn. But hers was one of those warm acquaintanceships born of Twitter. Her handle, @CleverTitleTK, often appeared in my Twitter stream, and we had engaged with each other over the years in a way native to our cultural moment. A decade earlier, such a relationship would have made no sense. A decade hence, Twitter might well be obsolete, replaced by another mode of rapid-fire communication. But in June 2016, it was simple enough for me to direct-message @CleverTitleTK, whose brief Twitter bio read: *Old school journo. Genealogy geek.*

Michael had known of Jennifer Mendelsohn's subspecialty in genealogy because when Ancestry.com returned his own altogether unsurprising results, it turned out that the two of them were distantly related. He had shown up on her page as a fourth, maybe fifth cousin. During an email exchange, he learned the depth of her interest and knowledge of these testing sites.

"She might be able to help us—maybe there's another level of information here I can't access."

My phone pinged almost instantly. It was @CleverTitleTK sending her phone number.

13

Indelible: the rumpled white sheets, their texture slightly nubby. The thin blanket pooled around my waist. Michael seated at the desk. Both of our laptops open. The coffee, room temperature at this point. I hadn't emerged from my cocoon—not to pee, not to brush my teeth. Jennifer Mendelsohn was on speakerphone. We had already walked her through the basics.

"Let's take a look at the family tree associated with this Thomas Bethany," she began, clicking on a link we hadn't been aware of.

"I didn't know you could do that."

"Got it. Here she is. Bethany Thomas."

"I knew it!" Michael seemed almost happy.

I typed "*Bethany Thomas*" into Facebook. There were five or six people with the same name.

"Wait, hold on. Now I've just gone on *her* family tree," Jennifer went on. "Her maiden name is Hort."

I searched for *Bethany Hort Thomas* on Facebook. Sure enough, there she was. The air was charged with a strange, dangerous momentum, as if I was nearing the top of a roller coaster. Our educated guesses had propelled the ride up—but we had no idea what would happen once we hurtled into the wild speed just on the other side of the crest.

I clicked on a blurry image of a middle-aged woman in a striped sweater. I saw instantly that we had no shared friends, had liked none of the same pages. I would never have stumbled across her. I scanned posts and photographs from a life very different from my own, scrolling down her page with a merciless intensity, like a stalker trailing a stranger down a busy street. Little kids in a bouncy house. A bunch of people cheering at a football game. Cute kitten photos. She seemed to live in Ohio. What was I looking for? Some way of identifying my first cousin A.T. I was crystal clear when it came to one piece of logic. Later, when I obsessively tell the details of this day dozens upon dozens of times—*the nature of trauma is that you have no recollection of it as a story*—people will look at me blankly when I get to this part. I'll have to break down this simple line of reasoning, one every family knows and takes for granted. If it was true, if A.T. was indeed my first cousin, then an uncle of his—either his father's brother or his mother's brother—would be my biological father.

"Here we go. Her husband's name is Adam Thomas."

Jennifer was moving even faster than we were. Adam Thomas. A.T.—Michael had been right. I kept scrolling down, my thumb against the keypad, scanning, scanning like a gambler at a slot machine until I arrived at a photograph of a man in his late fifties. Receding hairline. Round face. Glasses. Big smile. *With my husband Adam Thomas at our daughter Kaycee's wedding.*

"Does he look like Dani?" I heard Jennifer's voice from a great distance. "I don't think he looks like Dani."

From that moment forward I would have a uniquely intimate relationship with this journalist with whom I had never before spoken a word. The people who are with us by either happenstance or design during life-altering events become woven into the fabric of those events. The man who sat next to me on my flight home when my parents were in their car accident; the doctor who diagnosed our baby boy with a rare and frightening disease. I, too, have been that person in the lives of friends and strangers. And now @CleverTitleTK, the sister of a friend, would forever be part of our trio of detectives as we zeroed in on the seemingly impossible.

I had already moved on, frantically searching for Adam Thomas online, looking for information about his parents. It was a common name. So far I was coming up empty. If we found nothing, it proved nothing. But what if we found something? Someone? Ancestry.com—with its army of geneticists—put it at 98 percent that this Adam Thomas was my first cousin. How many uncles did he have? How could I find out? I felt no connection to this round-faced, smiling man. But he had the potential to be an arrow, pulled back tightly in its bow, aimed straight and true. Of course, none of this was a thought. I had no thoughts. I was all keen instinct. We never know who we will be in the burning building, the earthquake. We never know until we are faced with our own stripped-down, elemental selves. I wanted to flee. I wanted to stay. I wanted to rescue myself and the whole of my history.

"His mother died in 2010," said Jennifer Mendelsohn. She had searched for him along with his Ohio town and his wife's name. "Here's her obituary."

"Here we go," Michael said. He looked over at me from his seat at the desk, perhaps ten feet away. We somehow knew before we knew. My husband has always been a remarkably comforting presence for me. Whenever the world has seemed to shudder and tilt off its axis, Michael has made me feel safe. I have felt that, together, we can get through anything. But what was unfolding now was mine alone.

Jennifer began to read aloud. "Eloise Walden Thomas passed into eternal life . . . born in Cleveland, Ohio . . . a stay-at-home mother . . . her church was at the center of her life . . . surviving her are five children, twenty grandchildren, a sister, two brothers . . ."

Two brothers. *Surviving* brothers. The brothers of the mother of my first cousin.

"One of her brothers is a doctor who lives in Portland, Oregon," Jennifer continued. "His name is Benjamin Walden."

At the word—*doctor*—Michael and I gave each other a quick, startled glance. It was almost too easy. All we had been going on were a couple of key words. Hardly anything, really. Our hunch about a medical student. A mysterious first cousin with the initials A.T. And now this. An uncle of that first cousin. Who was a doctor. Who was alive.

Michael came over to the bed and sat next to me. It had been thirty-six hours since we had sat side by side on the chaise in my office—since I had discovered that my father hadn't been my father. *Dr. Benjamin Walden.* I entered his name, my fingers cold and shaking. *Benjamin Walden. Ben Walden. Dr. Ben Walden.*

There was no part of me that believed this was happening, even as it unfolded with a sense of inevitability so profound that I will later come to think of it as a kind of fate.

On the page for a medical website: *Dr. Ben Walden is a thoracic surgeon who retired from active practice in 2003. He is a well-respected speaker on the subject of medical ethics. He is a graduate of the medical school at the University of Pennsylvania.*

14

In the months to come—indeed, I suspect, for the rest of my life—I will hear stories. Friends will send me links to news items. Experts will share their experience. I'll be told of people who have searched for their sperm donors—their biological fathers—all their lives. When these searches have been unsuccessful, some have had their anonymous donors' identification numbers tattooed on their bodies, a way of marking themselves with their only clue. I've seen photos of arms, ankles, shoulders inked with stark series of numbers. And with each story of a dead end, a locked door, I am stunned anew. A favorite poem, "Otherwise" by Jane Kenyon, begins like this: "I got out of bed / on two strong legs. / It might have been / otherwise. I ate / cereal, sweet / milk, ripe, flawless / peach. It might / have been otherwise." The poet goes on to regard ways in which the bounty of her daily life contained within it the shadow of a darker possibility.

My daughter was conceived in Philadelphia, my mother had said that long-ago evening. *Not a pretty story.* When pressed, the word *institute.* Her language was precise. The thing she never planned to say—that slipped out on the second anniversary of my father's death, and only because I introduced her to my friend from Philadelphia—was an enormous piece of luck. What if that friend had been from Detroit? What if I hadn't brought my mother to the graduate student reading that night? A seam ripped open in my mother that night that allowed me access to a vital clue, though I didn't know it at the time. A moment, a split second—and then it closed up again. If she hadn't said those exact words—but if everything else had remained the same—when I got the results from Ancestry nearly thirty years later, I would have discovered that my father wasn't my biological father but known nothing more. I would have come to the conclusion that my mother must have had an affair. I would have supplied yet another false narrative to the story of my life.

What if Adam Thomas hadn't shown up on my Ancestry page? What then? All would have been yawning, cavernous emptiness. Devoid of possibility. Like the baby bird that fell from its nest, I might have wandered through the world never knowing where I came from. I would have been left with a hole inside me in the shape of a father or, rather, two fathers. The father who raised me, who died too young, too sad, too lost, and the anonymous man I came from but would never be able to identify. Instead of a false narrative, there would be an infinity of narratives.

Michael kicked off his sneakers and sat in bed next to me. My laptop was balanced between us as we waited for a YouTube ad to finish. Dr. Benjamin Walden. Five syllables—seven if you included the prefix. A nice mellifluous name. He had a website. It took three clicks to get there. It was a simple site, a repository of blog posts and essays he had written about medical ethics, along with links to a couple of videos. The screen went black, and then his name in white sans serif type appeared. Dr. Ben Walden speaking at Reed College, Portland, Oregon.

An old man with white hair and blue eyes was standing at a lectern.

"My god," I whispered.

Time slowed to a near standstill. I couldn't compute what I was seeing. Or rather, *who* I was seeing. The man was wearing khakis, a blue button-down shirt, and a fleece vest. He had a pale complexion, but his cheeks were pink, his color high. My exact coloring. Somewhere, in the background, the comments I had fielded just about every day for fifty-four years: *You sure you're Jewish? There's no way you're Jewish. Did your mother have an affair with the Swedish milkman?* I saw my jaw, my nose, my forehead and eyes. I heard something familiar in the timbre of his voice. It wasn't merely a resemblance. It was a *quality*. The way he held himself. His pattern of speech. He was recommending a book to the audience, Atul Gawande's *Being Mortal.* He referenced an article in *The Onion.* I had the bizarre thought that he had good literary taste. I ran my hands down the length of my legs. Who was I? *What* was I? I felt as if I might disintegrate right there in that hotel room floating high above the city. This wasn't what I wanted to see. But now that I had seen it, I would never be able to un-see it.

Dr. Ben Walden. His name continued to appear beneath the lectern. The glint of eyeglasses. A wedding ring. Michael raised the volume. The man's voice moved through me and around me like something invisible, stitched into the air. *In just a moment I'll open it up to questions—*

"Jesus," Michael was saying. "Jesus Christ."

Now, Ben Walden was gesticulating. He held both his

hands in front of him as if bracketing the air in parentheses—a gesture that I suddenly recognized as my own. I knew in a place beyond thought that I was seeing the truth—the answer to the unanswerable questions I had been exploring all my life. The audience in Portland was now raising their hands. He called on someone in the back row, then nodded, smiling slightly as he listened.

"Do you see that?" I asked Michael. "The way he's—"

"He even runs a Q and A like you," Michael said.

The following summer there will be a total eclipse of the sun, and Michael, Jacob, and I will take turns looking at it through NASA-approved glasses. But I will not trust the NASA-approved glasses. I will still look at the eclipse for only a fraction of a second at a time. This is the way I watched the YouTube video on that June morning. A glimpse, then away. Another glimpse. As if the old man in the blue button-down shirt and Patagonia vest—who he was and what that meant— might blind me forever.

15

I slipped out of bed and walked barefoot into the bathroom. My mind and body seemed to be disconnected. My body wasn't the body I had believed it to be for fifty-four years. My face wasn't my face. That's what it felt like. If my body wasn't my body and my face wasn't my face, who was I? In several weeks, once I'm back east, I'll meet my best friend from college for dinner, and when I walk into her apartment, I'll realize I'm afraid that her feelings for me will have somehow changed, that I am now unknowable to her. I'll stand in her living room, tears streaming down my face, and ask: "Do you still see me as the same person?" And she will look at me, bemused, compassionate. "You *are* the same person," she'll say.

But on that morning in Japantown, I encountered my own face in the mirror and understood for the first time that the information reflected back at me had always told a different story than the one I had believed—no, more than believed: known. I didn't feel like the same person. The white-haired, blue-eyed doctor from Portland was now staring back at me. He had always been staring back at me. And it wasn't only a physical thing, certain common features. Watching him on

YouTube, I felt with my entire being something I could barely understand. *Come from him.*

I wrapped myself in a robe and sat at the small desk where Michael had made the discovery about Bethany and Adam Thomas less than an hour earlier. I closed the tab for the YouTube video and opened my email:

To: Dr. Benjamin Walden
From: Dani Shapiro
Subject: Important Letter

It had been easy—just as everything else had been insanely easy—to find his contact information. He had a blog. He was out there in the world, a well-respected physician, a public speaker. He was a man who would probably have no reason to think his in-box would contain any huge surprises. How old was too old for a surprise? He was seventy-eight.

Dear Dr. Walden,
I'm writing to you about something that may come as a shock. My name is Dani Shapiro and I am a fifty-four-year-old novelist, memoirist, wife, and mother of a seventeen-year-old son. I live in Litchfield County, Connecticut. I recently took a DNA test as nothing more than a lark. I have always believed my parents to be my biological parents. But now I have reason to believe that you may be my biological father. I won't write more unless (a) this makes sense to you, and (b) you're willing to communicate with me about it. I so hope you're willing.

I'm going to send you a link to my website so you can see something of who I am: www.danishapiro .com.

Thank you.

Dani

Michael was in the shower. I waited—my finger hovering for a moment before I hit send. Before she got off the phone, Jennifer Mendelsohn had asked me what I was going to do, now that I had zeroed in on my biological father. She urged me to be methodical, to do research. Apparently there was a right way and a wrong way to go about this. There were, she told me, templates. But I wasn't feeling careful or methodical; in fact, quite the opposite. I was feeling wild and reckless. I needed not to sit back and cogitate but to take any and every kind of action. As long as I was in motion—my fingers against the keyboard, the pen across the page, dressing for the day, swiping lipstick across my now unfamiliar lips, strapping on my sandals—I was able to hold on to the belief that I was propelling myself forward, rather than falling backward into the abyss.

16

An early memory: it's a Saturday afternoon in the late 1960s and my parents are sitting with friends in our New Jersey back-yard. The flagstone patio is in dappled shade. A forsythia hedge spills over the next-door neighbor's fence. The adults sip iced tea from green plastic cups and relax on the kinds of lounge chairs that leave marks on your thighs when you stand. Maybe there's a bird feeder. I know this much: it's *Shabbos,* which means no cigarettes for my father, no radio for my mother. Lunch is served cold, as it always is after my dad returns from temple. The friends are named Kushner. Many years later, their son will be arrested and imprisoned in a tawdry case involving hookers and embezzlement. Their grandson will marry Ivanka Trump. But on this day, the Kushners are just nice older people, quite a bit older than my parents. I'm young—five or six—and when I come outside to say hello to the grown-ups, Mrs. Kushner pulls me to her side. She's a stout woman with a teased hairdo and a thick accent. I've heard whispers that she and her family dug a tunnel out of the Jewish ghetto in their Polish town during the war, enabling hundreds to escape. Mrs. Kushner runs her hand through my hair, which is white-blond, the same color as my eyebrows. She looks at me hard. What does she see? I am pale, blue-eyed, delicate. I have a heart-shaped face. She's still gripping me when she says: *We could have used you in the ghetto, little blondie. You could have gotten us bread from the Nazis.*

Fifty-two percent of Eastern European Ashkenazi descent. And the rest: French, Irish, English, German. A schism, a fault line, a split. Just about half of me could have, in fact, gotten bread from the Nazis. I was an Orthodox Jewish girl who had the *siddur* memorized, who belted out the *Birkat Hamazon* with my father after every *Shabbos* meal. I spoke flawless Hebrew—a language that now, when I hear it, has the quality of a half-remembered dream. But I didn't look the part—not just a little bit but to such a degree that it became a defining aspect of my identity.

I have very few childhood memories—really hardly any at all—but I have always remembered the backyard, the dappled shade, the green cups, and the lounge chairs that particular *Shabbos* afternoon. My father, still in his suit pants, tie removed, his shirtsleeves rolled up. An embroidered red velvet yarmulke covering his head. My mother is hazier—my mother is always hazier—but she certainly witnessed the moment with Mrs. Kushner as she sat at the table laden with sliced brisket and cold poached asparagus.

What was Mrs. Kushner really saying to me? What had she been thinking? I was being told: You're one of us. And I was also being told: You're not one of us. Which was it? And why has this memory stayed with me all my life? I've told the story of Mrs. Kushner before. I've written about it in essays and other memoirs. I thought the story's significance was the strangeness, the trauma of being told as a child that, had I been alive during the war, I could have saved people—and my guilt that I wasn't able to. But now I know that it was the kernel of truth embedded in that memory that kept it intact for me. Mrs. Kushner meant no harm as she gripped my arm and assessed me. She spoke without thinking and as she did, said what everyone thought when they looked at me. It was the first time I recall—though far from the last—that I was told I wasn't who I believed myself to be.

Once, in my twenties, I actually kept a log of how many times I heard that I didn't look Jewish in a single day. *Shapiro your married name? I've never seen a Jewish girl who looks like you.* At times, it troubled and angered me. What did it mean, to not "look" Jewish? Certainly there were plenty of blond, blue-eyed Jews. The comments struck me as veiled anti-Semitism when they came from non-Jews, and self-hating when spoken by Jews. What was most uncomfortable—but also a potent and shameful source of secret pride—was that I understood that it was often meant as a compliment. I was pretty in a way that couldn't possibly be Jewish. Pretty in a 48 percent French, Irish, English, German way, as it turns out.

This is what Jewish looks like, I would think, a kind of internal fuck you. I led with being Jewish wherever I went in the world. It was like a parlor trick, something guaranteed to produce interest, even amazement. *You, Jewish? No way.* And I would respond by dutifully reciting my family's *yichis,* a Yiddish word that translates to wellborn. I would reel off my credentials: *went to a yeshiva. Raised Orthodox. Yep, kosher. Two sinks, two dishwashers, the whole deal.*

17

And something I *didn't* remember, not until I was reminded of it eight months after that morning in Japantown. I had traveled to Washington, D.C., to attend a large annual writers' conference where I ran into an old friend whom I hadn't seen since we were in our twenties. As we stood in the cavernous, crowded exhibition hall, we caught up about kids, husbands, books, teaching. It never occurred to me to share my recent discovery with her. It wasn't the time or place, and besides, we hardly even knew each other anymore. Just before I was about to move on to the next booth, she referred back to the long-ago summer when we first met as young writers with fellowships to Bread Loaf, a conference in Middlebury, Vermont.

"When I think of you, I think of one particular night," she said. "A bunch of us were sitting around a picnic table after dinner—the fellows and the faculty—do you remember?"

She paused and looked at me searchingly. The faculty at Bread Loaf was made up of literary giants. A few of the fellows had since gone on to become giants themselves. Had something happened that night?

"Mark Strand stared at you across the table and said, *You aren't Jewish*. He declared it. Like it was a fact. In front of everybody. He wouldn't let it go. He just kept staring. *You aren't Jewish. There's no possibility you're Jewish.*"

My old friend's words sank in, and the noise of the D.C. conference hall receded around me as if someone had just hit the mute button. The familiar refrain now meant something altogether different, and no part of me could shrug it off.

"There was such an edge to it," she went on. "He was a *poet,* a man who knew precisely the value and import of language. He was totally aware of the impact of his words. It was like he was stripping you of who you were. He just kept repeating it over and over again. He got angrier and angrier, as if he thought you were lying."

If pressed, I wouldn't have been able to place myself at that picnic table. Whatever had happened that night was buried beneath layers of cotton wool. Nor would I have been able to say for certain that I had ever met Mark Strand. I could picture his craggy, handsome face. He looked a bit like Clint Eastwood. He was a romantic figure, Poet Laureate of the United States, a hero of mine. Just recently I had come across a photograph on Instagram of Strand's grave in upstate New York. His tombstone, polished but left rough on top, was stark against the snow. MARK STRAND, POET. 1934–2014. He died at eighty. Across the bottom of the tombstone, a line from a poem of his own: WHEREVER I AM, I AM WHAT IS MISSING.

"I've never forgotten that moment," my friend said. "You were so poised in your response to him. You didn't give away what you must have been feeling. I wondered what that poise was costing you."

"I don't recall any of this," I said softly.

Little blondie.

.   .   .

As it turned out, Mark Strand knew something about me that I didn't know. He set his gaze on me as if applying a contour map. It wasn't just my blond hair and blue eyes. No—this had to do with angles, bone structure, skin tone—this was data that didn't add up. My dismissal of that clearly offended him. Here was a highly perceptive person—a poet I admired to such a degree that I later used a line from a poem of his as an epigraph to one of my novels—demanding that I take a good hard look at myself.

How was it that I had never suspected? Not even after my mother had let slip the method of my conception? I was in my early thirties that summer at Bread Loaf. It had been only a half dozen years since Susie had told me about the practice of mixing sperm. It seems a sliver of doubt would have wedged itself within me. But there was no doubt. No suspicion. I staunchly ignored the evidence. Instead, I sat, glib and certain under the starry Vermont sky, incurious about why this kept happening, why Mark Strand felt moved to speak with such conviction.

Story of my life was what I usually said with a shrug and a sigh. A phrase that seemed to cost me nothing. *Story of my life.*

18

I had a full day ahead of me in San Francisco. I suppose I could have canceled my long-scheduled lunch and our evening plans, but what was I going to do instead? Climb back into bed? If I stayed in the hotel room, I knew what would happen. I would check my email every five minutes, hoping to receive a reply from Benjamin Walden. I would probably do that anyway, but at least I'd be on the move. Who knew how long it would take him to write back—that is, if he was ever going to write back? Maybe he was out of the country. Or had fallen ill. Or maybe we were wrong, completely wrong about him, about everything. Was it possible? I kept asking Michael whether there was still some chance that all this was a crazy hallucination, a bunch of coincidences arranged so that they only appeared to be facts.

But this was shock talking. This is what shock does. The trapped, frozen mind looks to rearrange the data. In a recursive loop, I kept drifting back to the beginning: the Ancestry .com results, Philadelphia, A.T., Bethany Thomas, University of Pennsylvania, medical student, Ben Walden. I pored over the long-ago conversation with my mother, mining it for further clues. I could hardly bear to think of my father. To think of my father would bring him close to me, and then he'd be able to see what was going on. This is how my thinking went. I didn't want to break my dead father's heart.

Michael and I wandered through the sprawling structure called the Japan Center next to our hotel. Even in mid-morning, the place was filled with tourists. Japanese families snapped photos beneath the five-story concrete Peace Pagoda. We walked the length of the indoor mall, past Japanese, Chinese, Korean restaurants, boutiques. A hair salon, a bakery. In a paper goods store, I combed the aisles, looking for the perfect notebook. Writers tend to be fetishistic about our materials, and I am no exception. Spiral-bound, perfect-bound, lined, unlined, pocket-size—as if the notebook itself might make a difference. Instead, I ended up buying the packages of index cards, understanding something I couldn't have articulated: my life was now in fragments I would need to shuffle and reshuffle in any attempt to make sense of it.

My lunch date was with a friend whom I hadn't seen since she'd moved to the West Coast a couple of years earlier. We were meeting at a vegan restaurant in the Mission. When I had made plans with her, weeks ago, I thought we'd cover the usual subjects: work, family, politics, gossip. Now, the conversation was probably going to go a little differently. How could I talk about what was happening to me? How could I *not*?

In the back of a taxi on my way to the Mission, I checked my phone. I had five new emails, and as I scrolled through them I felt a disconcerting emptiness. It had been two hours since

I'd sent the note to Benjamin Walden. He lived in Portland. We were in the same time zone. Wouldn't he have checked his email by now? I was insanely, unreasonably impatient. *Refresh, refresh.*

I imagined a home in the Pacific Northwest—just a short flight from where I now stood on the corner of Valencia and Mission. I pictured the old man with white hair and blue eyes wearing khakis and a fleece. Perhaps at that very moment, he was pulling a chair up to his desk, which was covered with papers and medical journals. By his side, a steaming earthenware mug of tea. There would be a picture window behind the desk that overlooked a backyard shaded by aspen and poplar trees. As a novelist, the characters I create are as real to me as the people in my everyday life. But this was no character. The noise in my head was so loud I wondered if it might travel all the way from San Francisco to Portland. Maybe just then Benjamin Walden was powering on his desktop computer and opening his email, scanning past fund-raising requests from the Democrats (it seemed all but certain that he was a Democrat), notices from his golf club (he looked like a golfer), and stopping at an email with the subject line *Important Letter*.

The restaurant my friend had chosen for our lunch was called Gracias Madre. The irony of the name didn't strike me, and it isn't until a year later when I try to piece together the events of that day that I look back in my calendar and can't help but laugh. *Gracias Madre*. As I floated, dizzy and spectral as a junkie, down Mission on my way to the restaurant, it wasn't my mother who was on my mind—and certainly I wasn't in the mood to thank her. I had decided, if anything that day can be called a decision, that my parents had been completely in the dark about the circumstances of my conception. It had been an accident. A mistake. Or maybe a betrayal of them by someone at the institute. My parents had spent their lives not knowing, same as me. No other explanation was bearable.

19

A cool façade got me through the day. The inner avalanche was somehow not apparent on the outside—this had always been the case with me. I held myself together even as I worried that I might pass out. I told my friend the story over lunch at Gracias Madre, aware that I was recounting it, not feeling it. I heard the words coming out of my mouth, I registered her kind, stricken face across the table, but part of me had levitated and was now hovering, as if the story weren't my own.

This hovering continued that evening in San Francisco. Dinner had been planned months in advance with a couple we adored. The evening, as we had envisioned it, would be boozy, fun, a celebration of friendship. As Michael and I walked from our hotel to their Pacific Heights town house, I continued to fidget with my phone. The whole day had gone by without word from Benjamin Walden. Maybe he wouldn't write me back. But if he didn't write me back, wasn't that a certain kind of proof? *Dear Ms. Shapiro, I'm sorry but you're mistaken. Dear Ms. Shapiro, I was never a sperm donor. Dear Ms. Shapiro, You're out of your fucking mind.*

What I remember: a marvelous, fairy-tale house, the front parlor where we gathered for drinks before heading out to a bistro a few blocks away. A vodka martini with two olives in a long-stemmed glass. I had texted earlier that day to let them know that I had, as I put it, seismic news. It seemed an appropriate choice of words. It was San Francisco, after all. *Good seismic or bad seismic?* the wife had written back. *Just seismic.* They looked at us expectantly. What was the news? Michael and I found ourselves tag-teaming the story as if we were actors in a play—a darkly comedic play—tripping over one another, mining the story, beat by dramatic beat. The vodka was having the desired effect. I was becoming numb, but also voluble. It was a good story. A great story. I had pretty much lost sight of the fact that it was *my* story. We had them laughing. We had them on the edges of their seats. We spent most of the evening talking about it, over steak frites and good French wine.

The next day I received a text: *Any word from the good doctor?* The wife's tone was breezy and dismissive, unlike her. She was usually highly sensitive, tuned in. I had begun to despair about ever hearing from Benjamin Walden. I had double- and triple-checked his email address to be sure I had gotten it right. Of course, this was absurd. What was I thinking? That Benjamin Walden would leap to respond to what must have been a bombshell? But as I careened through the hours, I had no patience, no capacity to be measured. The good doctor was my biological father. Meanwhile, the texts continued. *Keep us posted with updates!* I was hurt by her tone. How could she not understand that this wasn't a soap opera, this was my life? But later, much later, I came to understand that I had presented it as entertainment. So had Michael. It was a default and a defense; if we were able to shape it into a story, perhaps it would hurt less.

That night, a second night we had planned—a dinner party in the fairy-tale house—I went in resolved that I wasn't going to say a word. I wasn't going to hijack their evening. It wasn't their fault that my life had blown up. It was a table of extraordinary raconteurs, and for whole minutes at a time, I was able to forget that the ground beneath me had cracked wide open. I ate the seafood paella, drank more than my share of wine. I laughed, told other, easier stories, clinked glasses. I met Michael's eyes across the table. *I've got you,* those eyes said.

It continued to seem oddly possible to go on living my life as if nothing had happened. Nothing had, in fact, happened. It had been uncovered, but it wasn't new. It had always been the case. My father had never been my father. A doctor from Portland had always been my father. I was not who I thought I had been. But I was who I had always been.

The next morning, when I awoke, I could wait no longer. Certainly, I should have given it more than two days. The templates Jennifer Mendelsohn had spoken of would have me waiting weeks, months, possibly forever. Eventually, I'll read sample letters online—generally meant for parents of donor-conceived children who wish to contact their anonymous sperm donors—that contain phrases like *priceless gift* and *unbelievably lucky and grateful.* Experts counsel patience. *If you receive no response at all you must respect the donor's wish for privacy. When breaking the barrier of silence with your child's donor, be sincere and stay hopeful.*

To: Dr. Benjamin Walden
From: Dani Shapiro
Subject: Regarding my letter

Dear Dr. Walden,
I realize my letter must have been shocking to
you and respect that you may need to process this
information before deciding how to respond. I'd be
grateful, though, just to know that you received it.
I'm reeling from this myself. It has turned the entire
narrative of my life upside down. Of course, if you
haven't received it, I'll resend.

Thanks. I hope to hear from you.
Dani

20

To: Dani Shapiro
From: Dr. Benjamin Walden
Subject: re: Regarding my letter

Dear Ms. Shapiro,
I apologize for the delay answering. We were out
of town plus it's taking some time to process the
information you sent. I have shared this with my
wife and we are thinking this over. We now reside
in a retirement community and are enjoying our
children and grandchildren. If you wish to send more
information, we'll be glad to review it.
　　Best regards,
　　Ben Walden

As a girl, I wasn't allowed to study Talmud, the ancient collection of texts in which rabbis and scholars explored and dissected the meaning of every word in the Old Testament. The
word itself, *talmud,* means to learn. As the boys read the Talmud, we girls studied the less-interesting *Dinim,* which were
the laws themselves. Still, I credit my yeshiva education with a

love I've always had for parsing language. I read Ben Walden's email aloud to Michael as we packed up our hotel room in Japantown. It arrived two hours after I had sent the inappropriately prodding, non-template follow-up. I felt a powerful and immediate sense of vindication. I had so little to go on—nothing but instincts—and my instincts thus far hadn't led me astray. The good doctor had responded to my simple, human plea.

I noticed that he used the word *plus,* rather than *and.* I didn't know what it signified, except that it was an interesting linguistic choice. *Shared this with my wife. Thinking this over.* It could mean only one thing: he had indeed been a sperm donor. The math added up for him. Seventy-eight minus fifty-four equals twenty-four. Minus nine months equals twenty-three. The age he would have been as a young medical student at Penn. I purposely hadn't included details—Farris Institute, University of Pennsylvania—in my initial letter to him. I had asked him if it made sense, and this was his response. Yes. Yes it made sense.

We now reside in a retirement community and are enjoying our children and grandchildren. I interpreted this as a request, even though he had asked me for nothing. *Don't disrupt our lives* was the subtext pulsing just beneath those words. *Don't hurt us.* How old was too old for a surprise? And then finally, that they—Ben Walden and his wife—would gladly review any further information I sent. The pronoun, throughout: *we.*

I had included a link to my website in that first letter. This, too, I did for a reason. I may have been in a feral state when I composed it—an animal bent on survival—but within that state I had a survivor's clarity. I wanted him to see that this woman claiming to be his biological child was not crazy. She wasn't after his money. Her public persona, at least, was one of a relatively sane and successful person. She had written quite a few books. She had taught at an Ivy League university. She seemed like someone he might even be proud to have fathered.

There was a wealth of information about me on my website. Links to all my books, to essays and stories I'd published over the years. I had a blog he could peruse if he so desired. And then there were photographs—author photos, and one in particular, the first one that he would have seen when he clicked on the link I had provided. In it, I'm standing behind a podium, giving a reading. My hair is pulled back, I'm wearing glasses, and I am his spitting image. It wouldn't have taken long for him to understand that the woman who had landed in his in-box, upending his life, claiming to be his biological daughter, was a writer who had spent her life trying to understand who she was and where she came from.

21

What did my mother know? What did my father know? And again:
What did my mother know? What did my father know? In yogic
philosophy the concept of *samskara*—the Sanskrit translates
into scar or pattern—is understood as a karmic inheritance, a
blueprint we're born with and cycle through again and again
over the course of our lives. As Michael and I made our way
down the West Coast, the wheel spun around and around, each
time catching in the same exact notch—the place of a thousand questions that really all could be reduced to the same two
questions. All the while, I scribbled on index cards:

Dystopia.
Feeling (then) as if I were under glass. Feeling that way
again now.
Speech from *Richard III* about nail in horseshoe.

Friends in Malibu were hosting a July Fourth party. We
watched fireworks on the beach. The widow of Dino De Lau-
rentiis had a new boyfriend, a retired pilot who was part of a
recreational squadron. They buzzed overhead—eight small

jets in formation against the purple California dusk. I composed a long, careful letter back to Benjamin Walden explaining the maze of facts that snapped together as if they had been magnetized. I kept my tone simple and clear, stripped of emotional content. We were now on a first-name basis. *Dear Ben. Best, Dani.* But whenever my unruly mind wasn't otherwise occupied, it returned to my parents.

Everyone involved in the story was either dead or very old. My parents were dead. Most of their friends were dead. My mother's sister—to whom she was very close—was dead. Her husband, a surgeon, was dead. Dr. Edmond Farris was dead. Farris's wife, Augusta, was dead. The Farris Institute had been shuttered a decade after my birth. But I was aware that there might still be living people who could shed light on what happened in that institute in Philadelphia that led to my conception. Doctors, nurses, clinicians, or technicians who had worked at Farris. Professors at Penn who might have known Farris himself. Colleagues in the then relatively new field of reproductive medicine. I didn't have the luxury of emotion recollected in tranquillity. My job now was to amass as much information as quickly as I possibly could. Conveniently, this job also meant I could keep the tidal wave of my feelings at bay as I waited for a reply from Ben Walden.

One article I came across was a widely circulated 1958 wire service story that appeared in newspapers such as *The Milwaukee Journal-Sentinel* and *The Tampa Tribune:*

Test-Tube Baby Practice Grows; Now 30,000 in U.S.

Some 40,000 American children owe their start in life to test tube science.

Dr. Edmond Farris, director of the Institute for Parenthood in Philadelphia, said in an interview that even his estimate of "30,000 to 40,000 test tube tots" may be low. No one really knows exactly how many test tube children there are in the U.S. because there is no law requiring doctors to report on this practice.

Dr. Farris is one of an unknown number of scientists quietly working in this field, although laws have never been enacted to control artificial insemination of humans.

Allen D. Holloway, Chicago lawyer, in a recent issue of the *Journal of the American Bar Assn.,* said that legislators should study the problem and adopt some uniform statute. He warned: "The act of artificial insemination involves criminal law, legitimacy, inheritance, and even spills over into the fields of theology, sociology and philosophy."

Dr. Farris, like his colleagues in the field, thus operates in a legal no-man's-land.

He is conscious of religious thinking too, but as he puts it: "I see nothing wrong in trying to bring children of fine quality into the world."

He described the donors in his institute as the "best material that Philadelphia medical schools can offer."

The whole procedure is handled in strictest confidence. Records are heavily coded to prevent information from getting into the hands of would-be blackmailers.

As an added precaution, the couple involved is instructed to be intimate before and after the test tube procedure. This, according to a leading obstetrician, leaves the matter of the "real" father open to speculation.

22

By the time Michael and I picked Jacob up at UCLA to take him to dinner, it had been four days since I'd discovered that a retired doctor in Portland was my father. The main reason for our trip to the West Coast had been to visit Jacob midway through his summer film program. He'd never been so far away from home for so long. But I was thankful that Jacob hadn't been around. I wasn't ready to break this news to him. I had no idea how he would feel about it. I had no idea how *I* felt about it. I continued to seesaw between painful clarity and incomprehension about my entire history. My son was the only other person in the world for whom this discovery had genetic significance. All my life I had been giving medical history that was 50 percent incorrect. *Father: dead. Family history: heart disease, stroke, depression, alcoholism (paternal uncle), drug addiction (father), anxiety disorder.* I had been carrying burdens that weren't mine. I was careful with alcohol. I worried when I had a heart palpitation. But what was starker and more upsetting was that I had also been unwittingly supplying incorrect medical information for my own son. When he was stricken with a deadly disease as an infant—a seizure disorder so rare that its origins were unknown—I confidently told the doctors that there was no history of seizures in my family. But was that true? Had there been? An entirely different genetic world existed within me—and within my son.

Jacob was excited to tell Michael and me all about his film program, the scripts he was writing, the short film he was making. It was easy to sit back and just watch him. He fit right in to the candlelit Hollywood restaurant with its palm fronds and comfortable banquettes. Seventeen, sandy-haired, lithe, with a Roman nose and deep blue eyes—he was a gorgeous boy, and I was, had always been, besotted with him. Maybe because we had come so close to losing him when he was small, I never took him, or anything about his existence, for granted. So many times I had wished my father and Jacob could have known each other. I conjured up the ease and friendship they might have had—both of them sensitive, kind, thoughtful, honest men. I was also comforted—I now realized with a start—by the thought that something of my father continued to live on in Jacob. Susie had no children. After me, Jacob was the last genetic link to my dad. I had always searched for my dad in his face, and his mannerisms. If Jacob had children of his own someday, there would, in some small way, be a tiny bit of Paul Shapiro continuing on in the world. This felt, though I never could have articulated it, like something I had done right.

Pru u'rvu. Be fruitful and multiply, and fill the world. The first words God spoke to human beings in Genesis. They were apparently more important than the commandments not to steal, or kill, or lie. *Pru u'rvu.* The first mitzvah. Had it given me pleasure to think of Jacob as my father's descendant because I knew how important that would have been to my father himself? Now, as I sat across the table from my son, I felt heartbroken—not for him, not for me, but for my dad.

Beneath the palm fronds, as our waiter cleared desserts, I gave my phone a quick glance—always a reflexive habit, but more so these days than ever. I drew a sharp breath when I saw that Ben Walden had answered my last email.

From: Dr. Benjamin Walden
To: Dani Shapiro
Re: Important Letter

Thanks for the information. I'm forever amazed by the power of the Internet. Your research may be correct. I may plan to have DNA testing to evaluate this. I'm very grateful that you will respect our privacy and are not interested in disrupting our family.

First of all, congratulations on a very successful writing career. My wife and I plan to read your memoir. If the DNA findings show a match, I would imagine that you would be interested in some family history especially any medical history. If you let me know the questions you have, I'll try to respond.

23

Each time I felt strong and resolved enough, I typed various search terms into Google. *Sperm donor. Donor conceived. Donor anonymity. Ethics of donor anonymity. History of sperm donation.* I ordered all sorts of books, which would be waiting for me back home, packages stacked on our front porch. I already had a pile of articles from the 1940s through the early 1960s about Dr. Edmond Farris. I could hardly bring myself to read them. The language was archaic and devastating, like something from a science fiction comic book. *Test tube tots.* Was that what I once was?

There seemed to be communal outrage about donor insemination in the years surrounding my conception. Ethicists, religious scholars, lawyers, even many physicians believed it to be unlawful and immoral. At the same time, there was a smug certainty on the part of the doctors and scientists at the forefront of donor insemination. Secrecy, anonymity, and even eugenics were discussed in a matter-of-fact way. Donors were chosen for their perceived genetic superiority. Records, heavily coded, were sealed or destroyed. Parents were told to go home and forget it ever happened.

But the language of contemporary reproductive medicine was no easier to contemplate. As I scrolled through websites and online essays, words swam; sentences broke apart. In every other area of my life I was capable of clear thought. But here, I was back in the thick sludge. It became quickly apparent that the community of the donor-conceived was robust and active. I stumbled upon words I hated: apparently Ben Walden was my *bio-dad*. Paul Shapiro was my *social dad*. The phrases made me feel like a freak of science. But then I read that being donor-conceived often made people feel like freaks of science. One website offered special jewelry: *Conceived just for you!* Parent-on-a-chain necklaces fashioned out of aluminum, chrome, or brass, on which hung dog-tag–shaped charms customized with donor numbers. I wanted to hold myself apart, as if none of this really applied to me. The understanding that this world was *my* world, that I was donor-conceived, that this was indeed (and had always been) a term that applied to me, rose up like a concrete wall I slammed into again and again.

One name kept appearing on research papers, websites, even on Oprah: Wendy Kramer. She had created something called the Donor Sibling Registry, a resource for donor-conceived people who were out there desperately searching for their genetic relatives. I found myself wanting to reach out to Wendy Kramer—but why? I didn't need her services. I had already found my biological father. Ben Walden didn't occupy the deepest, most tender part of my attention. What I wanted: confirmation from someone—an expert—that it was possible, no, more than possible, likely, no, more than likely, *absolutely the case,* that my parents had known nothing. The Farris Institute had hoodwinked them. Gone rogue. Someone must have decided it would be in this couple's best interest to add donor sperm to the mix without telling them. Maybe the institute was trying to increase its success rates. Or Dr. Edmond Farris had decided to play God.

Our last couple of days in Los Angeles were taken up with work meetings, more visits with Jacob, as well as lunches, coffee dates, drinks dates, and dinners with friends in that sprawling city that was, in many ways, a second home to us. Sometimes I told the story, and sometimes I didn't. I had begun to learn that telling it didn't necessarily make me feel better. Increasingly, I found that as I recited the narrative it became amorphous, the vastness of it like an echo chamber. I would feel my mouth move, hear the words as if someone else were speaking them. I grew quieter and quieter. I was dreading going home. I kept thinking of our house with its walls covered with portraits of my ancestors. My writing office, where I had surrounded myself with them: my grandmother, grandfather, my father and Aunt Shirley as children. I pictured a bucket of paint and wanted to whitewash the entire interior. A blank slate.

Finally I wrote to Wendy Kramer. Each time I wrote a new person in this strange, unfamiliar world, I felt exposed and vulnerable. But I encountered nothing but kindness from those I contacted to ask for help. Kramer got back to me within minutes. We made a phone date to speak that afternoon. At the appointed time, I wandered Wilshire Boulevard, looking for a quiet place to talk. I stopped at a nail salon that had a small metal table with two chairs on the sidewalk out front, and asked the proprietors if they minded my sitting there. In the bright yellow-white light of the Los Angeles afternoon, I organized my materials as if I was reporting any old story: notebook, pen, noise-canceling earbuds in place. Just as I dialed Kramer, a woman came with her bagged lunch and plopped herself at the small table next to me. I stared at her as she unwrapped her sandwich. She did not meet my eye. *Fine,* I thought. I had no time to find a more private perch.

Kramer was warm, direct, and entirely unhurried. As I walked her through the details of my discovery—trying to ignore my tablemate—I wondered how many times she had been on the receiving end of such calls. The Donor Sibling Registry had close to fifty thousand members. Anyone doing even a rudimentary online search would land on her website, where her contact information was listed.

"You realize how unusual it is that you found your donor," she said. "And so quickly."

I did understand. Kramer's entire website was devoted to those searching, often fruitlessly. I was dimly aware of my own gratitude. I had already been supplied with a massive piece of the puzzle, even if I never had any further contact with Ben Walden. I knew who he was. I had seen his face. I had heard his voice. I knew where I came from.

"Do you ever hear stories like mine?" I asked her. "People in their forties and fifties who never knew—"

"All the time," Kramer responded. "And more and more. People are doing DNA testing just for kicks, and getting the shock of their lives. There was such a culture of secrecy. Sometimes the mother tells after the father has died. Other times, there's a letter left in a safe-deposit box."

I watched the passing cars on Wilshire Boulevard. My tablemate showed no sign of leaving.

"But I'm sure my parents didn't know," I said to Kramer.

"I think Farris must have used a donor without my parents' knowledge."

There was a brief pause on her end.

"Why do you think that?"

I had begun to explore the *halachah,* the body of Jewish law, as it pertained to the subject of donor insemination. It wasn't just forbidden; it was considered an abomination. The word nauseated me. *Abomination.* Did this mean that I was an abomination? According to Jewish law, the sperm donor would have paternity. Not the infertile father. *Your father is still your father.* Not according to the rabbis.

"My father was an observant Jew," I said to Kramer. "He would never have been okay with not knowing if a child of his was Jewish."

That was what my mother had said, wasn't it? The sentence remained indelible, preserved for all these years. Later, Michael will point out to me that my mother had not, in fact, answered the question I had asked. She simply posed another question in response. And further, her choice of words was striking. Wouldn't know the child was Jewish. As opposed to: wouldn't know the child was his.

"Your parents had to know," Kramer said.

My tablemate scraped her chair back and stood, slowly gathering her trash.

"It's out of the question," I responded.

I hunched over my notebook, scribbling. Trying to get our conversation down, so that I could attempt to understand it later. The very idea was unthinkable. I mean that literally. I was unable to entertain on any level the thought that my parents had known all our shared lives. That they had purposefully deceived me, withheld from me such an essential truth.

That they had looked at me—their only child—with the awareness that I had not come from the two of them but had been fathered by an anonymous medical student. There had to be another explanation—one in which a nefarious doctor had duped them. I clung to the only story I could tolerate. A few days earlier, a wise friend, the Buddhist teacher Sylvia Boorstein, had told me that my present state reminded her of a particular illustration in Antoine de Saint-Exupéry's *The Little Prince*. At first glance, the illustration appears to be of a big green hat. But on closer examination, it becomes clear that a boa constrictor has swallowed an elephant. I was that snake. Choking on the elephant.

"Well, your mother had to know," Kramer said.

I wondered why she was so sure. She didn't strike me as the kind of person who would issue forceful opinions for no reason. I thought of my mother, her simmering fury. Her ownership of me. Her condescension toward my father. Was it possible? Could my mother have orchestrated my conception without my father's permission?

"The mother always knew," Kramer went on. "I've spoken to thousands of donor-conceived people. I've heard thousands of stories. I'm not saying it's impossible—but I've never heard a story in which the mother didn't know."

24

Another memory, or perhaps less a memory than something vestigial, now pulled from the ruins of my childhood. Just as I can feel Mrs. Kushner's hand on my shoulder, just as I can see my mother's profile illuminated by the lights of the George Washington Bridge, so another moment comes to me whole: I am three years old, and my mother has brought me from our New Jersey home into New York City, where the well-known children's photographer Josef Schneider is going to take my portrait. It isn't the first time I've been in front of Schneider's lens, though it is the first time I have any recollection of it. My mother knows him from back when she worked in advertising, before she married my father. His background as a child psychologist makes him uniquely suited to photographing young children. He is adept at eliciting certain moods and expressions from them, and—if all else fails—he bribes them with candy.

Snap! Schneider makes faces at me. He thinks I don't know that he's holding a button in his fist that is making the shutter snap. *Snap!* My mother must be close by, watching. I've just looked it up, and Schneider's studio was on West Fifty-seventh

Street. There may be faint city sounds from the busy street below. The sigh of buses, the wail of sirens, honking horns. *Smile, Dani! Over here, Dani!* Something tells me that this is important to my mother. That I had better perform, and perform well. *That's right, Dani!* She would have pronounced my name, as she always did, as if it were slightly foreign and exotic, drawing out the *a. Daaah-ni.*

I have very few memories of my early life, but this—the shutter, the button in the photographer's fist, the sound of my mother calling my name—is one of them. Schneider wasn't just a portrait photographer. He had been responsible for discovering the babies who were in the commercials and ads for everything from Ivory Snow to Pampers. He recruited babies and children from everywhere: agents, managers, proud mothers, even hospitals. I recently dug up a profile of him in a 1977 issue of *People.* "You're lucky if you get one good baby out of fifteen," he sighed to the reporter. "A kid is as individual as a thumbprint."

The portrait from that day's shoot became the holiday poster—the *Christmas* poster—for Kodak that winter. In it, I am set against a pitch-black background, and wearing a black pinafore over a puffy-sleeved white blouse. The pinafore is decorated with a deep red poppy. My hair is cut into Dutch boy bangs, and I am playing with a wooden train that carries a half dozen red and green wooden elves. I appear solemn, quizzical, as I focus on a point just above the camera's lens.

The way my mother always told the story, the Kodak people—clients of Schneider's—just happened to be visiting his studio shortly after he had taken my portrait, and had asked if it might be possible to use my image on the poster for their national campaign. My parents agreed, and that winter a massive Colorama billboard dominated the main terminal concourse of Grand Central Terminal. A poster hung on a wall at F.A.O. Schwarz for years. Ads were spotted by family and friends all over America.

As I recall, it was a source of great merriment in our home: the fact that an Orthodox child was out there wishing the entire nation a very Merry Christmas. Such a hilarious accident! My mother loved to tell it: she had brought me to the city for a commissioned portrait and, instead, the executives at Kodak had discovered me. A framed version of the poster had a place of pride in the living room of my childhood home, where anyone visiting would be sure to see it. Beneath my quizzical face is a whimsical illustration of a couple being pulled through a snow-covered field on a horse-drawn sleigh.

Confirmation bias—a psychological term I had never heard before but one with which I will become intimately familiar—is the process by which the mind seeks to confirm what it already believes. When in the throes of confirmation bias, we seek and interpret information that will allow us to continue to hold on to our beliefs, even when presented with contradictory evidence.

You aren't Jewish, Mark Strand had flatly said.

We could have used you in the ghetto. Mrs. Kushner ran her hand through my hair.

Raised kosher, I replied more times than I can count. *Went to a yeshiva. Spoke fluent Hebrew.* And when faced with the bemusement, the disbelief: *I know. It's crazy. I mean, I was the Kodak Christmas poster child.*

· · ·

Once back home in Connecticut, one afternoon Michael stood for a long time staring at the Christmas poster, which now hangs in Jacob's bathroom.

"This was shot as a Christmas ad," he finally said.

"What do you mean?"

"You're playing with red and green elves," Michael said. "Look at them."

I stood next to him, examining the photograph of me that had been a part of my life's narrative for as long as I could remember, and for the first time registered the truth of what I was seeing. It was unmistakable. The elves' red and green hats were shaped like Christmas trees. The colors of the portrait were Christmas colors, down to the black and red dress I wore. It was not a portrait commissioned by a Jewish mother from New Jersey. It was a portrait deliberately shot as a Christmas ad.

"Are there any other pictures of you wearing that dress?" Michael asked.

No. No, there were not.

Perhaps Josef Schneider called my mother to suggest she bring me in to audition for the Kodak ad. Or it is also quite possible that my mother proffered me herself. She had disdain for stage mothers, so never could have admitted to such a thing. But given the opportunity, she could not have resisted the lure, the temptation of the spotlight. Her daughter, her hard-won daughter, her only child—so surprisingly pretty, so shockingly fair—beheld as the classic, iconic American child. As she returned home from the city, her mind must have worked overtime to fashion a series of lies my father would believe. My mother was quite convincing when she had set her sights on something she wanted badly. "Paul, you'll never believe what happened! The Kodak people want to put Dani on their holiday poster! Wouldn't that be so funny?"

Her unsteady gaze, her wide, practiced smile. Her self-consciousness, the way every word seemed rehearsed. His stooped shoulders, the downward turn of his mouth. The way he was never quite present. Her rage. His sorrow. Her brittleness. His fragility. Their screaming fights. The harsh exchange of whispers behind their closed bedroom door. As a child—not much older than I was when I played with the elves and the red and green train—I pressed my ear to that door. I strained to listen. *Your parents had to know,* Wendy Kramer said. *Your mother had to know.* My mother is buried in a cemetery near the Jersey shore. My father's bones lie in the Shapiro family plot in Bensonhurst, Brooklyn. And I am straining to listen now.

25

The hottest summer on record became my season of carefully crafted letters. I stayed indoors in the coolest, darkest room in my house, drafting odd requests and entreaties. The first of these was to Haskel Lookstein, a well-respected New York City rabbi who had known my dad. I let him know in an email that I'd made a stunning discovery about my paternity and was hoping to speak with him about the *halachah,* an area he was uniquely suited to discuss with me.

The week I wrote Rabbi Lookstein followed on the heels of his involvement in a controversy. He had been invited to deliver the benediction at the Republican National Convention, and his acceptance of the invitation had caused uproar among many members of his Upper East Side synagogue. Though he had changed his mind about offering the benediction, he was probably still dealing with the fallout. As I sent him an email, I wondered if he'd have the energy to meet with me. He was eighty-four years old. But I didn't have long to wait. I heard back from him that same day, inviting me to visit him in his office at the Ramaz School, the yeshiva founded by his father.

The morning of my meeting with the rabbi, I scoured my closet for my most modest skirt. It was a sweltering day. My longest summer skirt hit me two inches above the knee. My shoulders had to be covered too. I checked my reflection in my bedroom mirror, turning this way and that, beset by a feeling of not-quite-rightness. It was familiar—this sense of being inappropriate that came upon me whenever I entered observant society.

The city sidewalks outside Rabbi Lookstein's office shimmered. Two double-parked trucks had created a bottleneck on the corner of Lexington Avenue and Eighty-fifth Street. I was early for my appointment and stood in the shade of an awning across from the entrance to Ramaz. Once again, I was dizzy, light-headed. I jumped at the sound of a jackhammer. I was nervous about meeting with Lookstein. He would have been a young rabbi at the time my parents were making their trips to Philadelphia. Was it possible that my father had consulted with him on the *halachah*? That the rabbi had direct knowledge about the circumstances of my conception? Or not. Maybe Lookstein knew nothing at all, because my father had known nothing at all.

Part of my father's history resided within the red-brick building abutting the ornate synagogue across the street. He would have attended services at Kehilath Jeshurun with his first wife, Susie's mother. I could picture them, a handsome couple, entering the arched doors in their Sabbath finest. Perhaps he would also have gone to services there with his second wife, Dorothy, before her illness took its final turn. It was only with my mother that my father left the fold, moved to New Jersey so they could begin anew.

It had always been true that in synagogues, when I heard

the melodies and language of certain prayers and songs, I would hear my father's voice, close to my ear, as if he hadn't been gone for decades. *Adon olam, asher malach.* I would sense his presence in these sanctuaries where he had felt most at home. I could hear him now, as I stood no more than a hundred yards from the closed doors of Kehilath Jeshurun. I could feel the smooth, worn fabric of his *tallis,* the silky fringes I played with when I was very young. *B'terem kol, y'tzir nivra.* How could it have been that I felt so close to my father but not at home in his world?

I was buzzed in by the security guard and slowly climbed the steps to Lookstein's office. The building was hushed, quiet. School wasn't in session. Seated in the receptionist's area, I leafed through copies of *Eretz* magazine. I pulled my phone from my bag and texted Michael. *My longest skirt is the shortest skirt in the building.*

Rabbi Lookstein was a slight man with a trim white beard. He invited me into his cluttered, book-lined office. On the far wall behind his desk was a portrait of Joseph Soloveitchik, another beloved Orthodox rabbi who had been close to my family. Soloveitchik was considered by many to have been the greatest leader of Modern Orthodoxy in the twentieth century. On the floor near the door was a huge blowup photo of Lookstein wearing a Mets jersey and cap, standing by the dugout at Citi Field. One of the team's owners was probably a congregant.

He seated himself in a chair facing me.

"I think I know why you're here," he began.

He did? All I had told him was that an issue had arisen about my paternity. What could he have gleaned from that? I braced myself for whatever he was about to say.

"Your mother had a first marriage before your father," he went on. "And you're worried that she never received a proper *get*."

A *get* is a Jewish divorce. The rabbi had thought about this. What other issue could I possibly have been bringing to him? At that moment, I realized that Lookstein knew nothing. There was no memory, no ethical dilemma about whether to be honest about a long-ago conversation. I felt flooded with relief. How desperate I was to believe that my father had been in the dark right alongside me.

"Um . . . no," I replied. "It's a bit more complicated than that."

I launched into the story I'd learned to tell without feeling the shock of its impact. I began with my DNA results.

"I'm not even sure that *halachah* recognizes DNA results," he interrupted. But as I proceeded, he grew quiet and listened carefully, his hands folded in his lap.

When I finished—telling him only the salient details, leaving out my correspondence with Ben Walden, which seemed, in that context, like a betrayal of my father—he nodded and stroked his beard.

"What concerns you most?" he finally asked.

After managing to keep my feelings tamped down, suddenly I was crying. "Whether my father knew," I answered. "The *halachah*—it seems so unlikely that he would have gone through with it. Whether my mother deceived him, or—"

"You'll never know," the rabbi said.

You don't know who you're dealing with, I thought but didn't say. *You'll never know* was unacceptable. *You'll never know* simply could not be what I was left with in the end. Who was I without my history?

Lookstein gave me a long, searching look.

"Which story would ease your heart?" he asked.

"The true one," I answered.

"No matter what, you're Jewish," he said. "Your mother was Jewish. Jewish egg, Jewish woman giving birth, the child would be Jewish. There would have been no need to convert you."

None of this had occurred to me, nor would it have mattered. One of the more minor surprises thus far had been how little I seemed to care about my acceptability as a Jew.

"And your son is Jewish. No issue there. Jewish mother, Jewish son." He said this kindly, as if offering me relief.

"But do you have any sense of whether my father would have sought rabbinic advice?" I asked. "And what you—or another rabbi—would have told him?"

Lookstein had the sad brown eyes of a basset hound, set in an elegant, elfin face. He crossed his legs, touched two fingers to his lips. His eyes traveled to the portrait of Joseph Soloveitchik behind his desk.

"*Kol hakavod* to your father," he suddenly said. *All the honor.* "If, god forbid, I had been in that situation myself, and my wife very badly wanted a child, I would have agreed to it."

"What are you saying?" My stomach roiled. The room expanded and contracted like an accordion. "Are you saying you think he knew?"

"Yes," Lookstein said.

"But the *halachah*—"

"I would give your father the *credit* that he wanted your mother to bear a child. He would have been fulfilling the mitzvah of *pru u'rvu*—the first thing God said to Abraham. Be fruitful and multiply."

I couldn't keep this version of the story in my head. My mother's logic, now rendered moot. It couldn't be true. My father had been many things. He had been fearful, terribly anxious. At times he'd had a temper. He was prone to depression. But he was an honest man. Could an honest man keep the truth of his daughter's origins from her?

"So you're telling me that my father would have proceeded with total acceptance?"

"What I'm telling you," Lookstein said, "is that he would have felt he had done a huge mitzvah."

I left Ramaz with the rabbi, and we headed west to Park Avenue. His head was covered by a straw fedora, and he clasped his hands behind him as he walked. I was less steady on my feet than a man in his mid-eighties. I didn't believe this story. I wasn't even sure Lookstein believed this story. I thought back to his first words to me: You'll never know.

The bright sun beat down on us. Every few moments a passerby greeted him and he tipped his hat. *Hello, Rabbi. Good afternoon, Rabbi.* This square block was his fiefdom. Was he just trying to make me feel better? Was it his rabbinic judgment that easing my heart was all that mattered?

"This was a more difficult question than the one I thought you'd have," he said. "If you send me your phone number, I wish to speak with a friend—the chief rabbi of Jerusalem—who might have further thoughts on the *halachah*."

As we rounded the corner of Park Avenue, Lookstein spoke fondly of my father. It was comforting to be in the presence of someone who had known him. There were so few people left. Lookstein and my father had been part of the same circle during all those years before he met my mother. When I had written my piece for *The New Yorker* about my father's ill-fated marriage to Dorothy, I had interviewed Lookstein's sister, who had been married to my dad's best friend. That tight-knit group of young people in postwar Manhattan seemed to have lived contented lives shaped by ritual and faith. But my father had been unlucky within all that simple contentment. Divorced. Then widowed. The great Lubavitcher Rebbe Menachem Schneerson himself had counseled my father to postpone the wedding until Dorothy died, but he couldn't bring himself to hurt her. Instead, he moved forward with an indelible action that carried with it agonizing consequences. He took a short, harsh journey on behalf of the woman he loved.

Lookstein nodded and tipped his hat as we parted on the corner of Eighty-fourth and Park. Was it my imagination, or were his eyes brimming with tears?

"We thought your father was a hero," he said.

26

I returned again and again with renewed astonishment to the thirty-six hours that had elapsed from the moment I discovered my father wasn't my biological father until the moment Ben Walden appeared on my computer screen. Thirty-six hours. Like a video I saw of an Australian kid solving a Rubik's Cube in 7.36 seconds. Impossible, but not. I would never be tempted to get a tattoo of my donor's number. I would never order a parent-on-a-chain dog tag necklace. I was lucky.

Ben was alive. Healthy. Not very old. And at least for the moment, he was willing to engage with me. But what—exactly—did I want from him? Ben Walden was not the deepest part of the story for me. He was not the end of the mystery but rather, the beginning. My visit with Rabbi Lookstein had not eased my heart. In fact, it had confused me further. I rewrote my own history repeatedly until the contents of my mind resembled a chalkboard, words not entirely erased, all smudged a cloudy white. Had my mother lied? Had the doctor covered it up? Why else would my father have raced to Philadelphia? But then there was Lookstein. *Kol hakavod.* Everywhere I looked, there seemed another possible set of circumstances. And each set of circumstances painted my past in a different light.

I dove into the books and printouts of articles from old magazines and scholarly journals that were stacked on my office floor, my bedside table, the kitchen counter—*Lethal Secrets, Artificial Insemination, Personhood Revisited*—in an attempt to understand the culture that my parents inhabited. In 1961, Edward Albee's eviscerating play about a childless couple, *Who's Afraid of Virginia Woolf?,* was about to open on Broadway. A *Newsweek* survey revealed that zero percent of Americans considered no children the ideal family size. What state of desperation would my parents have found themselves in? And what actions might have arisen from that desperation? A 2010 paper titled "My Daddy's Name Is Donor" painted a vivid picture:

> Donor conception has always been shrouded in secrecy. Anonymity is the thick cloth that permits no one to look inside. For years, the medical profession has touted anonymity as the answer to the quandaries created by sperm and egg donation. Anonymity protects the donor from having to confront the inconvenient truth that a child might be born from his or her own body. It protects parents who do not wish for an "outside" party to intrude on their family, and who quite often choose not to tell their children. And it certainly facilitates the buying and selling of sperm and eggs as products, no longer identified with one wholly unique human being whose life continues to evolve long after the "donation" is made. As a director of one of the oldest sperm banks in the U.S. said, "[Without anonymity], you're going to lose the really smart, the really wonderful people who I think are going to question, . . . 'Do I really want to

be in a situation where, down the road, someone may contact me?'"

Ben's communication with me was careful. I had the sense that each email had been combed over by multiple people—his wife, perhaps his children. One of his sons was an attorney. I had never before been in the role of being someone's worst nightmare, but I was pretty sure this was the case now. Ben was a good man, an ethical man. He could have blown me off. Ghosted me. Thus far he had been responsive, but surely he wasn't happy about the biological child who had appeared out of nowhere to disrupt his life.

Back in San Francisco, I had told Michael that if I had confirmation that Ben was my biological father, along with important medical history, I would be okay. It was more than most people got. I had seen his face. I had been able to watch him in motion—to see his gestures, his smile. I knew where I came from. It would be enough. So when, early one morning, I opened an email from Ben containing just what I had hoped for—information about a rare hereditary eye condition he had discovered in his early seventies, along with assurances that there had been no cancer, heart disease, or Alzheimer's in his family—I should have felt relieved.

But there was something else, something I couldn't quite put my finger on. Ben had written that he'd decided not to take a DNA test because he didn't trust the privacy provisions on commercial testing sites. He told me that he had been discussing the whole situation with his wife and children. That his family wished privacy in this matter. *Situation. Matter.* And again, *privacy.* The words disturbed me, but beneath the disturbance was something I wasn't used to feeling. I walked through my days feeling weighed down by a peculiar, polarizing heaviness. I wanted to hide. It was shame, I realized. The Walden family wished privacy in the matter of me.

What more did I want? After all, I had been given the very information I thought would make me whole. Above all, I wanted to eradicate this terrible shame, this sense of being defective, alien, *other,* as if perhaps I never should have existed at all. It was why, I now realized, I had included my website in my original email to Ben. It wasn't only so that he could see that my motives weren't mercenary. *See?* I wanted to say. *I'm a real person—with a full, rich life, and a family of my own.* I wasn't just the product of some random morning in Philadelphia— possibly one among many such mornings—during which he masturbated into a cup, tucked his shirt back into his pants, pocketed a few dollars, and returned to anatomy class.

I understood that he didn't want to think about something so unseemly. He was a successful, erudite, grandfatherly gentleman. I also realized that he had become a donor under the cloak of secrecy, the thick veil of anonymity that had been pervasive at the time. In 1961 it had been only nine years since Watson and Crick had discovered DNA. The thought of a future in which it would be possible to spit into a plastic vial and discover one's genetic heritage would have been the stuff of science fiction.

But here I was. An inconvenient truth that had indeed been born from his own body. A consequence of his actions. A wholly unique human being whose life continued to evolve long after his "donation" was made. My very existence was due to the fact that he never dreamt he'd have to deal with such a thing. And what I wished for now—though I knew expressing it might topple our entire parsed, careful dialogue—was to meet him. To be in the presence, just once, of this man I came from. *Be careful,* Wendy Kramer had cautioned. *He's a doctor. He's used to being in control. Keep your foot in the door. Let him call the shots.*

I waited until midsummer before writing Ben Walden with my request. I told him I'd fly to Portland for a cup of coffee. That I'd do whatever would make him feel most comfortable. I imagined sitting across from him at a café—Portland was a city full of cafés—and looking into his eyes, so like my own. I had watched his YouTube video perhaps a dozen times, each time struck anew by the similarities between us. I wanted nothing from him beyond this. I reassured him that I would continue to be respectful of his privacy. I hoped he would give this one-time meeting serious consideration. It would go a long way toward making the surreal real.

To: Dani Shapiro
From: Dr. Benjamin Walden
Re: re: re: Important Letter

Dear Dani,
Thanks for your very thoughtful note. I'm still trying to get my head around the fact that I have a biological daughter unknown to me for 54 years.

At the moment, my life is very busy and I'm still processing your request. It will take me some time to respond thoughtfully. So I'll write back in a few weeks to let you know my thinking (as filtered through my family input).

All the best,
Ben

27

It was time to tell Jacob. He had just returned from his summer program and was settling back into life at home. I hadn't wanted to give him this strange news while he was still in California, in case it would be upsetting to him. But I couldn't withhold it any longer. I had raised him without secrets—perhaps to a fault. I had grown up in a house where the air crackled with the unsaid. I had always wished for Jacob to feel that, in his home, the air was clear.

As I considered how and when to tell Jacob, I wondered, as I had when we were with him in L.A., whether it would matter. What were genes, after all, to a seventeen-year-old boy? Michael had been focused on the idea that Jacob now had a different grandfather, a *living* grandfather. But would Jacob feel that Ben Walden was his grandfather? I doubted it.

Jacob had never known my dad—so would this feel like a loss to him? I thought about this as I cooked my son's favorite dinner—grilled steak, roasted broccoli, spaghetti with butter and grated Parmesan—as if a good meal might help.

Family dinner had been a cornerstone of our lives since Jacob was in his high chair. So much of my way of doing things had been a reaction to the choices my parents had made. I had always known that I had formed myself in opposition to my mother. But I hadn't realized to what degree I had designed our family life counter to the one I remembered. As a child, I had most often eaten dinner alone. Meals with my parents were always in the dining room. The house of my childhood was formal and cold. The home I had shared with Michael and Jacob for fifteen years was simple and warm. But more than anything, what I aimed for was ease. I wanted to laugh with my son. I wanted him to feel he could be honest with me. And just about nothing made me happier than seeing how close he was with his dad. They had a few passions in common—particularly music, and the Red Sox—and a dialogue that was all theirs.

Michael had a good-size family. His parents were still living and had always been a big part of Jacob's life. Jacob had uncles, aunts, and an assortment of cousins as well. It had been a source of sadness to me that I hadn't been able to give him the same. No grandparents, a half aunt who displayed little interest, and cousins who were black-hat Orthodox, with whom he shared nothing at all. I had made sure to encourage a relationship between Jacob and my father's younger sister, Shirley, who was unusually open-minded, despite her strict religious beliefs. The previous year we had gone to Chicago for a visit. But the threads connecting him to my family were few and fraying.

I thought back to Jacob's bar mitzvah. I had presented him with a blue velvet pouch containing my father's enormous, yellowed *tallis,* the same one I remembered playing with as a child in *shul*. It had dwarfed him, and my aunt Shirley had sent along a pair of silver, filigreed *tallis* clips to hold it together on his narrow frame.

Here's my father's tallis. *You wrap it around yourself like this. These clips were your great-grandfather's.*

I had felt, on that day nearly five years earlier, a sense of completion. My boy, enfolded in his grandfather's prayer shawl. A modern, eclectic service that I had worked hard to design, which reflected our family and also honored my dad and his legacy. Though my Orthodox relatives would not attend Jacob's bar mitzvah, I felt I had their blessing. I stood next to Jacob in front of our gathered family and friends and spoke of how proud his grandfather would have been of him. *L'dor vador.*

"Honey, there's something important we need to talk with you about."

Jacob was suddenly very focused as we sat down to dinner.

"Nothing's wrong," I added quickly. "You don't need to worry."

As I began to share the story with Jacob, it felt unlike any previous time I had recounted it. It mattered—whether he would be aware of it or not—it mattered to him. I was giving him a missing piece of his own history. Michael was across the table from me, quiet, listening as I went through the details: the DNA test, the strange results, the lack of a biological connection to Susie, the mysterious first cousin. The artificial insemination, the discovery of the young medical student from the University of Pennsylvania. My voice shook. I was trying not to cry. Telling Jacob that my father wasn't his grandfather felt like I was undoing the work of a lifetime, or perhaps several lifetimes.

Jacob reached over and took my hand once he understood. "Are you okay, Mom?"

His chair scraped back as he stood and came around the

table to hug me—my beautiful boy, who wouldn't exist if everything hadn't happened just as it did. The dogs hunted for scraps at our feet. As I held Jacob close, I kept reminding myself that everything I had built—my family, my personhood—was unaltered. My new knowledge changed both everything and nothing. My life was like one of those large and complicated jigsaw puzzles that, once finished, displayed a completely different image on the reverse side: a streetcar in San Francisco, the Golden Gate Bridge. Van Gogh's sunflowers, a self-portrait. Same puzzle pieces. Same materials. Same shape. Different picture.

As it slowly sank in, Jacob asked only a few questions—all of them about Ben.

"Is he alive?"

"Yes."

I hadn't told Jacob Ben's name. I didn't want him going upstairs to his room and heading down the Google rabbit hole. I also wanted to protect my son. I had no idea how Ben was ultimately going to respond to my request for that single cup of coffee.

He gave a nod.

"Are you going to meet him?"

"I don't know. I'd like to. I hope so."

"Can I meet him?"

"Let's see what happens."

I resisted the ridiculous urge to tell Jacob that his grandfather was still his grandfather. What could that possibly mean to him? My father was an abstraction, an ancestor to him—nothing more. All those stories, the *tallis,* the sepia photographs scattered around our house of the little boy in the bowler hat—those were important to me. But they held no more of a sense of reality for my son than the fables and fairy tales I'd read to him when he was a child.

Jacob sat back down at the table and began cutting up his steak. I was suddenly hungry myself, relieved that this conversation, which had been looming, was now behind us. I watched as he ate his dinner with the gusto of a teenager and wondered if he would always remember this evening, or if it would eventually fall into the category of weird, but no big deal. He seemed to be lost in thought as he ran a hand through his thick, dark blond hair. I waited to see if there was anything else he wanted to know, or if we were just going to move on to other subjects. The Red Sox had a game that night. He and Michael would probably watch after dinner.

He took a big sip of water, started to say something, then stopped.

"What? You know you can ask me anything."

His hand raked through his hair again.

"So, just wondering—does this mean maybe I won't end up bald?"

Michael and I burst out laughing. My father and grandfather had heads like cue balls. I hadn't known it had even occurred to Jacob that it was hereditary. Ben Walden, on the other hand, did indeed have an excellent head of hair.

"You probably won't end up bald, honey," I said, glad that he was able to crack a joke. "I hadn't considered that particular upside."

28

That very first night—as Michael sat in our kitchen searching for the words *institute* and *Philadelphia*—it had quickly become clear that my parents had had excellent options closer to home. Cornell's medical school was, at that time, still housed at New York Hospital. The Margaret Sanger Clinic was well known. And just an hour and a half north, in New Haven, Yale School of Medicine's department of reproductive endocrinology would have been considered the gold standard.

My mother prided herself on always choosing the best of the best—whether in clothing, furniture, art, or jewelry. When she was dying she felt compelled to tell me that the Armani jacket in her closet still had its tags on, and that the double string of pearls were particularly fine—and she had mentioned more than once that her Park Avenue obstetrician's office was lined with photographs of movie stars, signed with notes of thanks. She enjoyed thinking of herself in the company of Ava Gardner and Rita Hayworth. So how had my parents ended up at the Farris Institute for Parenthood? Was there something about Farris that was different from the others? Or perhaps my parents wanted to go farther afield, to avoid any chance of running into someone they knew?

My mother had taken pains to describe Edmond Farris as a world-famous doctor, a pioneer in his field. If this was the case, there was surprisingly little information available about his work. Michael and I had been able to ascertain that he'd begun his career at the Wistar Institute, a scientific research center housed at Penn, and had risen to the position of director. But in the mid-1950s, Farris had been summarily dismissed. It was at that point that a few small newspaper articles about his new institute began to appear. Not the stuff of world fame.

I finally came across a video interview of Leonard Hayflick, an elderly endocrinologist who had worked at Wistar, in which he mentioned Farris. Hayflick was eighty-eight, and I could find no email for him, only a phone number.

He answered the phone with a sharp *yes* in lieu of a hello.

"Is this Leonard Hayflick?"

"Who wants to know?"

I wasn't cut out for this kind of reporting. I stuttered out my name and reasons for calling him until he became convinced I wasn't a telemarketer. Once we were clear on why we were speaking, I asked him if he could give me background on Edmond Farris.

"I knew Farris at Wistar," Hayflick told me. "A strange little man. When did you say you were born?"

"Nineteen sixty-two."

"Impossible," he said. "His lab at Wistar no longer existed by then. He had been kicked out in the mid-1950s—he was performing artificial inseminations and the Church found out, there was press, the local bishops became involved, pressure built—"

"And then he opened his own institute," I told him. "The Farris Institute for Parenthood. Where I was conceived."

Hayflick had never heard of the institute, and he had trouble believing that Farris had continued to operate near the campus of Penn after his dismissal from Wistar. But about this much, I was certain. I was proof of it. I began to think that Hayflick wasn't going to be of much help to me, beyond a sense that Farris was unpopular, a renegade. Hayflick described him as a Napoleonic type—short but dynamic, with sharp elbows. Someone who had made a lot of enemies.

But then Hayflick began talking about the science—his area of expertise. It seemed that Farris was a pioneer in two divergent ways, both of which would turn out to have been of great importance to my parents. First, he had developed a method by which a woman's ovulation could be monitored.

"Wistar was world famous for its colony of albino, virgin female rats," Hayflick said.

Just when I thought the story couldn't possibly get weirder. For months after this conversation, white rats would populate my dreams.

"While Farris was at Wistar, he benefited from the rat colony at no cost to him. The morning urine specimens of women would be inoculated into the ovaries of the rats—and then, a couple of days later, the animals would be sacrificed so that the ovaries could be examined. If the veins were red and swelling, it would show the hormonal surge of the woman's ovulation."

But there was a second area in which Farris had broken new ground, according to Hayflick—who clearly hadn't liked him and was loath to credit him with any discovery. Farris was among the first, if not the first, in the field of reproductive medicine to consider the male as the possible reason for a couple's infertility.

"Sexism was profound," Hayflick said, "and it was always

assumed that it was the wife, not the husband, who was responsible for the infertility problem. But Farris looked at sperm specimens for low motility and poor morphology."

My parents. My mother, pushing forty. Trying, month after month, year after year, desperate to have a baby. When had her miscarriages occurred? Before—or during—their excursions to Philadelphia? And why had she miscarried, over and over again? The culture dictated that the problem lay with her. Plus, my father already had a child. So when they chose the Farris Institute for Parenthood, it would have likely been because of Farris's innovation. Perhaps my mother's Park Avenue obstetrician to the stars pressed a phone number into her palm. *Go see this doctor. I've heard he gets good results.* My mother's urine, injected into the ovaries of albino, virgin rats.

But at some point, perhaps even at their very first appointment, Farris would have evaluated my father's sperm as a matter of course. He had been writing academic papers about male infertility that had been infuriating the medical establishment since the 1940s. He would have looked through his microscope at a slide and determined just how unlikely it would be for this couple to have their own child.

An older mother. A subfertile father. A couple who could not fathom their future without a baby—without *their* baby. A scientist with sharp elbows and a Napoleon complex. An era in which doctors played God. In which religious leaders of every faith decreed donor insemination an abomination. In which—in legal terms—it was often considered adultery, and the child a bastard.

What course was invisibly charted for my parents after they crossed the threshold of that institute in Philadelphia? Did my father race in vain—believing he was doing everything possible to have his own child? I imagine him now as he leaves his job and takes the subway to Penn Station. He settles himself on the train to Philly and cracks open *The Wall Street Journal,* but he is distracted. His mind drifts to my mother, his bewildering, despairing wife. He must feel it is his fault. *Slow sperm.* So unlucky. Divorced. Widowed. Now this. He has told no one. He bears the journey toward making a family alone.

In a small room next to a laboratory where white rats are locked in their cages, my mother waits. She is capable of being very still, my mother, like a statue, with her hands clasped, her legs crossed, a small smile in place. She's going to have a baby, goddamnit. And—this much is certain—at some point a fair-haired, blue-eyed medical student is also present. Pains are taken to be sure that Ben Walden and my mother never cross paths, though he is probably no more than fifty feet away, in another room discreetly outfitted with old issues of *Playboy.* His sperm has to be fresh; time is of the essence. If his sperm is indeed to be mixed with my father's—whether my father is aware of it or not—the two men might even pass each other in the halls of the Farris Institute.

Dr. Edmond Farris knew the score. But did he explain it clearly to my mother and father? Did he tell them that their chances of having their own baby were next to nil? That there was good news—a ready solution—one that might be difficult to contemplate but would greatly increase their chances for success? The more I continued to learn, the less I trusted any story.

When I was growing up in suburban New Jersey, in a neighbor-hood of pretty homes built on well-tended, one-acre lots, two cars in the driveway, and families of three, four, even five kids, it was notable that I was an only child. Especially because my parents were older—I now wonder what people thought of the white-blond, pale girl who lived in the red-brick house on the corner. When people commented on the size of our family— which, amazingly, they did—my mother had a ready response. I can hear her voice as if she's here in the room as I write these words. She would turn her beautiful, darting eyes on me, and I would feel pride. *I may only have one, but I hit the jackpot,* she would say. As if it were a lottery. She had won me. I was her prize.

29

Until I was in my mid-thirties—I met Michael at thirty-four, and Jacob was born days after I turned thirty-seven—my inner world was defined and shaped by longing. This longing was vast, wide, and I was not able to put words to it. All I knew was what I felt, which was a constant, interior ache that propelled me. At times, I felt like a sleepwalker in my own life, moving to a strange choreography whose steps I knew by heart. I have now read interview after interview with donor-conceived people—particularly those whose origins were not disclosed to them—who describe this longing. This sense of being trapped on the other side of an invisible wall: separate, alone, cut off, and—worst of all—not knowing why.

During my childhood, this ache took on two forms: first, I snooped. Whenever my parents were out of the house, as my bored babysitter watched television or talked on the phone with her boyfriend, I would stealthily climb the stairs to my parents' bedroom and open their drawers and closets. Many children are curious about their parents' private lives, but my ritual bordered on obsession. I ran my fingertips over my mother's chiffon scarves folded delicately in tissue. Her scent—rather, a mélange of scents—wafted up from inside each drawer: gardenia, jasmine, orchid, sandalwood, oakmoss, vetiver. Beneath her bathroom sink, she stored dozens of unopened boxes of L'Air du Temps and Calèche, as if she was afraid of ever running out. Her jewelry drawer was locked, but I had located the key and explored her necklaces, bracelets, earrings, and pins whenever I could, as if clues to who my mother really was might be found amid the gems.

My parents slept, according to Orthodox tradition, in single beds that were pushed together and attached to one headboard but made separately, each with its own set of sheets and blankets. The religious reason for this had to do with the belief that a woman is unclean during her menstrual cycle and the couple shouldn't touch at all during this time. I would sit on the sea of my parents' two beds and look around their room. The heavy silk curtains, their bedside tables with their twin clocks, the needlepoint pillows with their tiny stitches, all seemed to hold some sort of elusive truth. Then, if I still had time, I would walk into each of their offices and rifle through the papers covering their desks, careful to leave no trace. It wasn't anything specific I was after. It was just a sense that something was out of reach—and if I could only find it, this terrible feeling of longing would go away. I'd have my answer to a question I couldn't even formulate.

My second response to the constant ache was to look for a new family. I didn't realize that this was what I was doing, of course. We had a small dog, a poodle, and I walked that dog around our neighborhood every chance I got. I took the same route each afternoon, and longer walks on weekends. The neighborhood streets were named after English locales: Exeter Way, Surrey Court, Westminster Avenue. But it was the identity of each family in each home that consumed me.

The Quentzels had four kids, the youngest of whom was my age. The dad was a dentist. The Markowitzes also were a family of six. The dad was a builder, and the mom was young—the mothers were all a lot younger than mine, I came to realize. The Wilfs, Pantirers, and Kushners were among the community of Holocaust survivors. The Topilows had three mostly grown children. The dad was an ophthalmologist. The boys were already in college. Lawns were littered with swings, jungle gyms, plastic recliners. Sprinklers sprayed gentle arcs back and forth. I knew the neighbors' cars and made a study of the patterns of their comings and goings. Once school let out each day, it seemed like the moms and kids gathered at home. The dads pulled into the driveways at dusk. As I lurked and watched, I was like an anthropologist studying a foreign culture. Another form of life was going on behind the closed doors of these homes—a different, easier, more comfortable life than what was happening in mine.

As a grown woman, a mother myself, I received a phone call one day from our across-the-street neighbor from long ago. She felt compelled to share a memory about my childhood. I took notes as I listened: *Alarm went off. Babysitter in the basement, didn't hear. You came running across the street. Scared, alone.* As she recounted the story, I remembered the loud clanging, my confusion, and running in my nightgown across the lawn to their house. I recalled the grass beneath my bare feet, the strangeness of being outside all by myself in my nightclothes. The entirety of my childhood formed around the memory, and I felt a sudden cavernous emptiness. *The next day I stopped your mother to tell her what had happened. She was always leaving. Going to the city. Parade of babysitters. I told her you had been frightened.*

She needed to be home more. Or at least hire someone more caring. She screamed at me, furious. How dare I tell her how to raise her child?

I did everything I could to flee my parents. It pains me to write these words. They were all I knew of the world. And yet, I walked that poor dog up and down those unfortunately named suburban streets in search of a family who would open their door and take me in. I now wonder what those people thought; whether they were curious about why I was always circling their block, pausing by their front walks—why I always seemed to be hanging around. Once invited in, I ate cookies at their kitchen tables, watched television in their dens, drank soda on their porches, quietly desperate to belong to what seemed a warm, enchanted circle.

Eventually, the sky would begin to darken and it would be time for me to go home. I'd let myself in through the back door and make my way upstairs to my room. There was no one to ask me why I had been gone so long, or where I had been. The antiseptic silence was suffocating in contrast to the messy, noisy world outside. By the time night fell, either my mother would have returned from whatever she did during the day or a babysitter would make me dinner to my mother's specifications.

Later, the garage door would open, my father returning from his job in the city. That was the sound I waited for— the electronic rumble of my father returning, then the brief bear hug that seemed to contain within it his warm and beautiful heart. I was afraid of my mother and wanted very little to do with her. She was not the locus of my longing. It wasn't another mother I was after when I went from house to house like a stray kitten. It wasn't siblings, either. I was a girl in search of a father—not because I didn't love my father but because my love couldn't save him. That younger man on the train to Philadelphia had become a middle-aged man crushed by an accumulation of secrets, losses, and the unsaid. My father was already gone.

30

Before summer came to an end, I forced myself to fly to Chicago to see my father's sister, Shirley. It was not a trip I wanted to make. In all the exploration I'd done thus far—my conversation with my mother's best friend, Charlotte; my visit to Rabbi Lookstein—nothing had terrified me as much as coming face-to-face with my beloved aunt. At first, I thought I'd never tell her—that at the age of ninety-three, this was something she didn't need to know. But Michael had pushed me. Shirley might know something, he'd said. And he had a point. She and my father had been very close. If he had confided in anyone—that is, if he'd had anything to confide—it might have been her.

I was alone in the backseat of a town car on the outskirts of Chicago, searching for signs of Jewish life. It felt like we had been driving for hours, though it had been no more than forty minutes. Strip malls gave way to the flat grid of a suburban neighborhood. The driver turned on Golda Meir Boulevard. I spied a kosher butcher, a yeshiva, a lone Hasid in a long black coat and black hat walking down a side street lined with ranch houses and split-levels. When Jacob and I had visited the year before, we had arrived in the dark. Through the tinted window I saw a woman wearing a wig, holding the hand of a small boy with *payes*. I knew that Shirley's house must be close. As I neared her home, I fought an overpowering urge to ask my driver to turn around and head back to the airport.

In the years after my father's death, Shirley and I had grown increasingly connected. We spoke by phone often, and many times she had told me that she'd promised my father she'd look out for me. Though Shirley was my father's younger sister, she had always been his protector, and he had turned to her in times of emotional peril. It was she he had called when he learned that his young fiancée was terminally ill. It was she to whom he had confessed, in later years, his unhappiness in his marriage to my mother. During the time that my father and mother struggled to have a baby, he might have unburdened himself to Shirley.

I was back to the same lurching, destabilizing fear that came over me each time I was about to speak with anyone who might, in an instant, illuminate the extent of my parents' actions and awareness. Just as when I'd spoken with Charlotte, and Rabbi Lookstein, the possibility existed that I would discover with absolute certainty that my parents had colluded to keep my identity a secret from me. Wendy Kramer had summarily dismissed my belief that my parents hadn't known. Or, at the very least, that my mother hadn't known. *Which story would ease your heart?* Lookstein had asked me. *The true one,* I had answered. But at any moment, the truth could flatten me.

On the flight to Chicago, I went over some correspondence I'd had with the author of a dissertation on the history of fertility. *As for records, most clinics purposefully destroyed them,* she wrote. I stared at the word *destroyed,* willing the letters to rearrange themselves. I still held out the hope that a dusty file cabinet in the basement archives of Penn, or in the attic of one of Edmond Farris's three children, would contain notes, signatures, evidence. *In holding with psychological theories of the time, men were usually told to forget that the procedure had ever happened if they used a donor.* Could my father—could any father—have forgotten that the procedure had ever happened?

My car pulled away and I walked up the front steps to my cousin Joanne's home, where Shirley now lived. Another car would pick me up in four hours. Four hours, in which I would tell my aunt—who had once described herself to me as a weaver's daughter—that she and I were not threads in the same tapestry; that we were not related by blood; that her much-adored older brother was not my father.

Joanne opened the door and ushered me inside warmly. I was still holding a Starbucks cup from the airport. Was Starbucks kosher enough? I wasn't sure.

"Is this okay?" I gestured to the cup.

If it wasn't, she didn't embarrass me.

"Of course. Mom's been expecting you."

Joanne led me into a sitting room. There, in the corner, was a framed photograph of Joseph Soloveitchik, the same rabbi whose portrait graced Lookstein's office at Ramaz. A desk was surrounded by bookcases filled with leather-bound Hebrew volumes. On several long polished tables—just as had been the case in Shirley's home near Boston and in my grandmother's apartment in New York City—there were literally hundreds of family photographs. Perhaps as the eldest daughter, Joanne had inherited them. Being a part of this vast array had always comforted me, even as it had confused me. I was the lone pale, blond child in the sea of dark-haired, dark-eyed grandchildren and great-grandchildren—my otherness and difference glaringly evident. Yet I had never had any doubt that I was part of the chain that reached back and back through the generations, unbroken. As I stood in my cousin Joanne's sitting room, now knowing better, it felt as if the links of that chain were in pieces on the floor all around me.

Shirley emerged from her living quarters behind the sitting room, and we held each other close. She wore a dark skirt and a gray silk blouse, her silver hair pulled back into a low bun. She was unadorned. No makeup. No necklace, no earrings. Her plain gold wedding ring the only decoration on her elegant, supple hands. A Juilliard-trained pianist, she had still been able to sit at the keyboard and play Brahms ballades well into her eighties.

She had become smaller with each passing year. As I hugged her, the top of her head rested beneath my chin.

"Come into my room, sweetheart, before we sit down. There's something I want to show you."

I followed Shirley into her bedroom. She had managed to distill the contents of her seven-bedroom home near Boston into a simple, almost monastic space that still contained the essence of her life. Black-and-white portraits of her four children were arranged on a wall opposite her small, well-made bed. A photograph of her late husband, my uncle Moe, was crowded onto a bookshelf along with those of her two brothers, my dad and Uncle Harvey. All of them, gone. She was the last of her generation. A pair of ancient baby shoes sat atop a pile of Shakespeare plays. All of my books—five novels, three memoirs—were nestled among volumes of Judaica. My heart quickened as I had the devastating thought: Would she keep my books on her bookshelf, once she knew the truth? Would it matter to her—would she somehow blame me for not being her brother's daughter?

A laminated newspaper clipping from an advice column, old and yellowed, hung on the wall near the bedroom door. It seemed so out-of-place amid the religious artifacts in Shirley's room, in a place of prominence where she would see it each day as she left her living quarters.

> Q: You mentioned the poem James Garner recites in the Chevy Tahoe ad. Is it by e. e. cummings?—Fred Good, Mount Dora, Fla.
> A: "Nobody Knows It but Me" is by ad copywriter Patrick O'Leary. Many readers asked for the text. Here it is: "There's a place I travel when I want to roam, and nobody knows it but me. / The roads don't go there and the signs stay home, and nobody knows it but me. / It's far, far away and way, way afar. It's over the moon and the sea / and wherever you're going that's wherever you are. / And nobody knows it but me.

As Shirley rummaged through her desk drawers, I examined this unlikely bit of ad copy. Later, I would think about what the poem meant to Shirley. It was something apart and aside from her daily prayers. Something that was hers and hers alone, that seemed to go to the core of her spiritual life.

"I had it right here," she said, closing one drawer and opening another. "An envelope."

It occurred to me that maybe she was nervous. After all, I had called a few weeks earlier to say I had something important to discuss with her, and asked if I could pay a visit. She might have wondered why I was making the sudden day trip to Chicago. Or she might have suspected the reason. Either way, she would have been apprehensive.

"I wanted to give you—"

"Don't worry, Shirl."

"—wait, here it is."

I opened a small plain envelope and pulled out three photographs. One was of Jacob and me, taken on the beach in Cape Cod when he was a toddler. In the golden light and salty air, we look as alike as we ever will, our hair wild and wavy, eyes the same blue as the sea. I had sent it to Shirley years ago. Why was she returning it to me? I had the awful feeling that perhaps she really did know, and she was returning my own son to me, disclaiming him as part of the family. I shoved the thought away as hard as I could. And, not for the first time, I wished I had taken Michael up on his offer to accompany me on this trip.

The second two photographs were of my grandparents.

"I wanted you to have these of Grammy and Grandpa," Shirley said. "They were at the height of their ascendancy."

Height of their ascendancy. Who spoke in such a manner? And yet, coming from my aunt, it didn't sound odd but rather, like a humble statement of fact. It was no wonder I had mythologized my grandparents all my life. They were the stuff of myth.

Shirley and I settled on the sofa in the sitting room.

"I wonder if you know why I'm here," I began.

She shook her head no.

"I have a story to tell you, and I'm afraid you're going to find it painful," I continued.

Shirley was so small, her back erect as she readied herself to hear whatever it was I had come to say. Joanne must have gone out. The house was dead quiet—so quiet I heard a clock somewhere, ticking, ticking. Was there any part of her that had always wondered if this day of reckoning would come?

I began at the beginning. I told her I'd had my DNA tested. I looked for a flicker of awareness, a sense that she knew where this was going. I saw none. For the first time in my life, I understood the expression *blow by blow*. At the mention of an unfamiliar first cousin, a ripple crossed her forehead but nothing more. I began to explain about calling Susie and asking for her DNA sample.

"Do you need me to slow down?" I asked a couple of times. "Is there anything you don't understand so far?"

I asked this not because I thought she had the slightest cognitive decline. She had one of the sharpest minds of anyone I knew. But she was ninety-three. When she was born, automobiles were relatively new. Televisions did not exist. She was already the mother of four when Watson and Crick discovered the chemical structure of DNA. Another elderly person to whom I had recounted the story had asked: *So you're saying you're part your father and part someone else?*

Shirley grew ever more still as I spoke. She reminded me of a tiny animal in the forest: big eyes, big ears, quivering with attention. I told her that the comparison of DNA samples revealed that Susie and I were not related by blood. We were not half sisters.

She didn't move.

And then: "Shirl, did you know that my parents had a hard time conceiving me?"

"No, I didn't," she responded.

There it was—my answer. She hadn't known. If my father had kept a secret, he'd kept it from his sister as well. I went on to tell her about Philadelphia, the institute, my father's mad dashes from New York. As I spoke, a transcendent calm came over me. Some part of me broke off from the rest and marveled at this calm.

"So you're saying—"

"Dad isn't my biological father," I said. Five words. Five words and a lifetime. Her eyes were locked onto mine. I was afraid she was going to stop breathing. Not a blink. Not a sound. I feared it was as if I had said to her: *You're not mine. I'm not yours. We don't belong to each other.* It felt violent. The world around us fell away.

She leaned slightly forward, reached out, and grabbed my hand.

"I'm not giving you up," she said.

The thin shell holding me together cracked, and suddenly I was weeping with my whole body.

"And you'd better not be giving me up," she said.

Every syllable, deliberate.

"I'm not giving you up, Shirl," I sobbed. "I was so afraid that—"

"I have fewer years ahead of me than behind me," she said. "And you are my brother's daughter."

As the hours blurred together—coffee, bagels, lox, tea—Shirley entered with me into the thicket of what might have happened. I brought up the question of *halachah,* and she treated it as if it were completely beside the point, in the same way Rabbi Lookstein had. The two most religious people I'd consulted seemed willing to throw out the rulebook in this matter. She listened carefully as I shared Lookstein's opinion with her.

"It would have been within your father's character," she said slowly. "Very much in Paul's genre."

I repeated what Lookstein said about my dad and the choices he made back in 1953, when his young fiancée was dying. *Your father was a hero.*

"I think there was great nobility in what Paul did at that time," Shirley said. "The Lubavitcher Rebbe offered him a very easy moral out—to keep postponing the wedding until Dorothy died. When you're offered an easy moral out and you don't take it, that's *malchus.*"

Meaning *kingly.*

Grammy and Grandpa at the height of their ascendancy.

Great nobility.

My eyes had not stopped stinging with tears.

"Shirl, are you surprised that my father never said anything to you about their struggle with infertility?"

"Not at all," she said. "He would have felt private about it. That's something that would have been in the deepest interior of their marriage. He would have been protective of your mother."

A lifelong animosity had existed between Shirley and my mother. Shirley had described their relationship to me rather gently as being "on different wavelengths, as if there was electric circuitry buzzing in the wires between us." I recall hearing my mother's raised voice, the slamming down of a phone. But when I brought up the possibility that my mother had deceived my father—that he never knew—Shirley didn't go there with me. She preferred the version of the story that I found most painful: that my father knew all along.

"You're not an accident of history, Dani," Shirley said. Her eyes were brimming. "Not as far as I'm concerned and not as far as the world is concerned. This isn't about the cold scientific facts. I have to tell you—in every way, and I'm not saying it to make you feel good, and I'm taking a chance saying it because you'll think I'm making it up—but between you and Paul there *was* paternity, ownership, kinship."

She trained her whole ninety-three-year-old self, every cell in her being, in the direction of consoling me. Every bit of energy. It was the purest manifestation of love I had ever experienced.

"Knowing what you know, you're *more* of a daughter to Paul than you can possibly imagine. You take something that isn't your own and you breathe life into it. You create it—and it becomes your creation. You are an agent to help my brother express the finest kind of love."

Her hand rested on top of mine.

"It's rare that you get an opportunity in life to stand outside yourself. It's as if *Hakadosh baruch hu* is saying, *Child, come sit next to me and now, look.* Finding all this out is a door to discovering what a father really is. It isn't closure—you may not get to have that—but it's an opening to a whole new vista."

For the first time since that evening in June when I'd stared uncomprehendingly into my computer screen, I felt a sense of peace. At least for the moment, the constant ache was gone.

"You have to judge things by the result," Shirley continued. "And the result in which you can exult is that the very best was combined in you: grace, brains, creativity, beauty. Whatever alien, mechanical, outside element was in the story—it was a story of *success.* You have such a rich endowment. You have been so recompensed. You carry the heightened sensitivity, to be sure. You carry the pain and you also carry the reward."

Her voice—hoarse from speaking for hours—was a part of me. Her strong hands, her expressive forehead, her sweet smile—all a part of me, because she had always been a part of me. I had been so afraid that blood would be all that mattered. Oh, how I had underestimated my remarkable aunt. My car was waiting at the curb. She had hardly paused all afternoon. Her eyes had never left mine. Words had coursed through her as if channeled from the very God she believed in. *Hakadosh baruch hu.* She was telling me that she was still my aunt—that my father was still my father. My whole lost family encircled us as we sat in the fading light of her kitchen in Chicago.

"Sweetheart, this opens up a world of inclusiveness—and in the end, you have to include yourself. You aren't bleeding color. You're holding the light ones and the dark ones. They're all yours. Ultimately, in all of this, Dani—the postscript is that it's really called love."

Part Three

31

Shirley had used certain words to describe Ben Walden: *alien, mechanical, outside element. Cold scientific facts.* But Ben didn't feel like an outside element to me. Quite the opposite—he was very much an inside element. It wasn't just a physical resemblance. The man I watched on that YouTube video spoke in a cadence similar to mine, moved his hands in the same way, as if clearing space for his words when making a point. Donating sperm was not the same as, say, donating a kidney. Or a retina. It was the passing along of an essence that was inseparable from person-hood itself.

I had told Shirley nothing about discovering Ben. She didn't need to know that there was a retired doctor who lived in Portland—an actual human being with a face and a name—who was my biological father. *Knowing what you know, you're more of a daughter to Paul than you can possibly imagine.* I longed to believe this, even though I couldn't yet understand it. My father and I had shared a history, a culture, a landscape, a home, a language, an entire world. Our bond was real and unbreak-able. But I also now knew, in the starkest terms, what had been missing: mutual recognition. I did not come from him. I had never once looked into his face and seen my own.

Weeks passed as I waited, hoping for a response from Ben, who had asked for time to thoughtfully process my request. With each email exchange, I braced for the possibility that he might stop writing back. He could drop out of sight and there would be absolutely nothing I could do about it. Ben was the only person involved in my conception who was still living. My new reality continued to be ungraspable to me, and I was constantly aware of Ben's very aliveness—his existence on the other side of the country as he walked through his days, a person in the world.

I latched onto facts. It was a fact that I had been conceived by artificial insemination. It was a fact that my father wasn't my biological father. It was a fact that Adam Thomas was my first cousin. It was a fact that Ben was Adam Thomas's uncle. That he had been a young medical student at the University of Pennsylvania, where he had donated sperm. I ran through these facts as I tried to fall asleep each night, as if recounting them might help me make more sense of things. But what I was really doing was unspooling a narrative fifty-four years long, and perhaps meeting Ben would help me to find my footing, and to begin again, at the beginning.

As late summer's golden light fell across our meadow out back, I allowed myself to get caught up in fantasies of meeting Ben. I pictured a cool, crisp afternoon in Portland—a city that was a blank slate for me. I conjured up a café of Ben's choosing. Perhaps we would sit outside at a small table. It would be a one-time meeting—so I told myself—and that would be just fine. We would make polite small talk. Or we would speak of delicate matters. Maybe he'd tell me about the Farris Institute. Or maybe we'd stick with safer subjects. Try as I might, I couldn't imagine what it would feel like to see myself in a stranger. I wondered if he would, in fact, feel like a stranger. Michael asked me more than once what I hoped I'd get out of meeting Ben. I didn't know. I just knew that it felt urgent and necessary.

The books and printouts of articles and studies from scholarly journals and doctoral dissertations continued to pile up on my office floor near my desk. They shared the same small space decorated with the portrait of my grandmother, along with an entire crowd of framed family photos atop a standing bookcase. Each day I entered my office in a state of even deeper dread. The pile of paper grew, as my ability to tackle it diminished. I would begin reading an essay on, say, the legal history of donor insemination, and would find myself stricken, slightly ill, confused, enraged. I came across a *Time* cover story from 1945, "Artificial Bastards?," in which a judge ultimately ruled that artificial insemination is not adultery, and therefore not grounds for divorce. How had this become my story? Or rather, how had it been my story all along?

When I took a break from reading, I found it easier to search for more information about Ben on the Internet. Haunted by the eerie awareness that I was stalking, I scrolled through his blog on medical ethics, found bits and pieces of news about him and his family. He had been married for fifty years. His wife was a Brazilian nurse whom he'd met in the Peace Corps, just after medical school. I learned more about their three children: a girl and two boys. The girl—my half sister!—was only six years younger than me. I watched You-Tube videos of the Walden family at Christmas. A twinkling tree laden with ornaments dominated one corner of a living room. Tartan plaid place mats covered a holiday table. Teenagers ducked away from the camera. Little kids played underfoot. Grandparents sang a shaky duet that may have been a hymn. They were as foreign from my ancestors in the shtetl as could be. And yet they were—in the strict definition of the word—my ancestors. Who were these people? What did this family have to do with me? Once again I became that child standing outside the warmly lit houses of my neighbors, alone in the fading dusk, longing to be invited inside.

Early one Saturday evening, Michael and I were sitting in our library, about to head out to meet friends for dinner, when Ben Walden's name appeared in my in-box. As had been the case since the first time he wrote to me, the name—a name that would have meant nothing to me less than two months prior—filled me with a potent mixture of dread and excitement. I opened his email and saw that it was longer than the others. My voice shook as I began to read aloud to Michael:

To: Dani Shapiro
From: Benjamin Walden
Re: re: re: re: Important Letter

Dear Dani,
I truly appreciate your emails about respecting my family's privacy and I certainly take you at your word when you wrote, ". . . I would never expose you or your family in my work. I may someday write about my experience, but I will never name or identify you or your family. You have my word. That is not the kind of writer or person I am."
    I think I can understand and empathize with your desire to further connect face to face and to have further genetic confirmation of our link. I can only imagine how you feel since I've never been there

myself. A sense of our genetic link is important to most of us.

When I donated sperm as a twenty-two-year-old medical student, I was promised privacy and anonymity by the fertility institute so I, along with many medical student friends, became donors for a period of time. The thought of some future contacts from the children conceived by artificial insemination never crossed my mind. So this has been an unusual and surprising situation that I've given a lot of thought to.

I've looked though your website and read some of your writings. You are a remarkably talented writer and appear fortunate to be having such a successful career and family life. I'm happy for you in that you appear to be on a path to continue that success, which I hope brings you great personal happiness.

Dani, you have been able to see me from videos on my blog and to read my blog posts. These have bits and pieces of the biographical information I'm willing to share. Likewise, I have been able to see videos of you and to read some of your writings, so I feel I have at least some glimpse of your life.

At this point in my life, I don't have the time, energy, or interest to pursue this further. So, Dani, I don't intend to have genetic testing done or to have a meeting with you. I'm so sorry that this may sound harsh and uncaring, but I can't think of a better way to put it. I have reached this decision after discussion with my family and a few others. Please believe me; I empathize with your quest to understand your genetic history. But this is going to be my final communication with you. I wish you nothing but the best as your life moves forward with your family and your writing.

Best regards,
Ben

32

I stared at the last paragraph of Ben's letter. *Final communication. I'm so sorry that this may sound harsh.* I closed my laptop and sat there, trembling.

"He can't just do that," Michael said.

But of course he could. Ben Walden could do whatever he wished, his moral high ground the guarantee of anonymity given by a long-defunct fertility institute and the dead scientist who ran it. *Promised privacy. Many medical school friends. Period of time.* I didn't even need to refer to the letter—I had memorized it as I read it.

"He's scared," Michael went on. And this did seem possible. The tone of this letter was different from Ben's communication in the past. The repetition of my name, almost like a plea. *Leave me alone. Don't hurt me. Don't come after my family.* The quoting back to me of my own words about respecting his privacy—as if I might have forgotten them. The strange appeasement of his flattery, as if his praise of me as a writer might serve as some sort of consolation prize. And finally, the slammed door—quickly, almost in haste, as if he'd better act fast before he changed his mind.

I got up and poured myself a glass of wine. I had been drinking more than usual since late June, drinking differently—medicinally—blunting the internal blows. I took a deep breath and surveyed the room around me, trying to remember that I had a life that had been going on long before I knew about Ben Walden—a life in which the man in the yarmulke on the bookshelf was my one and only dad. A life in which the boy at his bar mitzvah was wrapped in the enormous *tallis* of his grandfather, fastened by his great-grandfather's filigreed *tallis* clips. A life of roots and certainty.

At first my fingers itched to respond. *I'm disappointed.* Or: *How dare you?* Or: *I hope you'll reconsider.* But instead of the wild, reckless abandon that had inspired my first communication with Ben, I now felt a calculating, merciless fury. I placed my laptop on the coffee table on top of a family photo album.

"I'm not writing back to him," I told Michael.

I wanted Ben's own words to echo in his ears—and I believed they might, even though I didn't know him. Even though he was a perfect stranger. He had shown himself to be a reflective person in each of our communications. And yet: *The thought of some future contacts from the children conceived by artificial insemination never crossed my mind.* In the fifty-plus years since he had been that young medical student, his brief stint as a sperm donor had not haunted him. He hadn't lain awake a single night wondering about the unknown children he might have fathered. Even when DNA testing became available—and later, when it became inexpensive and simple—the possibility of being sought out had never occurred to him.

But he was someone who spent his life thinking about medical ethics. And ultimately, this was an ethical question if there ever was one. What did I owe him? What did he owe me? Who were we to each other?

Michael and I left home and drove to our friends' place on a nearby lake. It was too late to cancel, and besides, what else was there to do? I seethed with a sense of futility and powerlessness. What if Ben really was resolved to keep the door between us slammed closed? I was an unpleasant aftereffect of an action so inconsequential to him that it didn't even bear recalling. A bit of space debris, the flotsam and jetsam resulting from a meaningless, young person's choice.

"Maybe this is it," I said to Michael as we drove the winding country roads, the pretty landscape in stark contrast to the darkness inside me. "Maybe there won't be anything more to learn. Not about my parents. Not about Ben."

"That's not what's going to happen," Michael responded. "No way."

"How do you know?"

"Too much has been set in motion. If nothing else—you know there are more half siblings out there."

Indeed, the likelihood of this was high. Very high. Ben had donated *for a period of time*. At that very moment there were probably half siblings of mine going about their lives, clueless. People who, like me, might have always been haunted by a feeling of otherness. Of not quite belonging. And the sense that there was something wrong—something secret.

So, there would be more to come. I knew Michael was right, that this wouldn't be the end of the story, but it didn't set my mind at ease. My biological father had made it clear that he was done with me. The possibility of half siblings conceived through artificial insemination was bizarre and felt somehow less than human, as if we had been a litter of kittens, each placed with a different owner.

A few days earlier, a high school friend had sent a photo she'd found of me, dancing at a sixteenth birthday party. I took in my pudgy, teenage face, my hair pulled back in a bandanna, my eyes half-closed in a self-conscious attempt to look cool and sexy. I remembered the disorder in my mind, my intense desire to please, my lack of any clear sense of myself. This is true of many teenagers, of course, but my relationship to my own identity was even murkier. That girl did not know who her father was. She was wrapped in a thick cocoon of the deepest sort of misinformation. She, quite literally, did not know where she came from. Would I ever again look at a photograph of myself, or my father, or my mother, without the eerie sense that our lives together had, from the start, been built on a lie? Would I ever look at myself and not see Ben Walden reflected back at me?

Late that night, half-drunk, exhausted, I created a new file on my computer titled "Imaginary Responses." In the weeks to come, each time I felt compelled to write to Ben, instead I would open the file and draft a note I knew I would never send:

IMAGINARY RESPONSE I

Ben,
For the rest of my life, when I look in the mirror,
I will see your face. As I'm sure you've noted,
the resemblance is more than striking. It would
have been nice to have felt better about the face
staring back at me. I wasn't asking for much, and I
gave you every assurance of privacy. I would have

happily signed a waiver or a release if that would
have made you feel better. For you to be unwilling
to grant me these two small favors which would
make a real difference in my life moving forward is
incomprehensible to me.

IMAGINARY RESPONSE 2

Dear Ben,
In one of my favorite short stories, Delmore
Schwartz's "In Dreams Become Responsibilities,"
written on the eve of his 21st birthday, a secondary
character addresses the narrator: "You will find that
out soon enough, everything you do matters too
much."

I would have thought that as a person whose
focus is on medical ethics, you would have considered
the ethics of the situation we find ourselves in, and
not fallen back on youth, or how so many others
were doing it, or a paper you signed at an institute,
promising privacy.

This is a moral, ethical, human issue. And though
I'm sure you have your reasons and can justify
them to yourself, you're doing something cruel
and inhumane, and not taking responsibility for
something you in fact did.

IMAGINARY RESPONSE 3

Dear Ben Walden,
I have begun referring to you in my head as Ben
Walden. Not Ben. Not "my biological father," which

is a mouthful. I need a way of thinking of you as the man who gave me life but isn't willing to meet me for a cup of coffee.

I feel it's important that I clarify one thing. It seems your greatest concern is your privacy. You've used that word in every single communication. Donating "for a period of time" is surely what you're most concerned about. I imagine you're worried that I'm at the lead of a long parade of offspring who will show up unannounced at your doorstep. Which of course is not my problem. I also imagine that you were worried, had you been willing to meet me, that I might have, say, Oprah jump out of the bushes with a camera crew. I wanted to reassure you that I would never have done such a thing, that my interest was—at its deepest level—in understanding where I come from, so that I might be able to live the rest of my life in peace.

33

The strangest summer of my life was coming to an end—though there were no signs that fall would be any less strange. Michael, Jacob, and I were getting ready for our annual trip to Province-town, on the tip of Cape Cod, to the artists' colony where I taught each August. I tried to focus on the ordinary, ground-ing details of daily life. There were lists to be made, of course. Always lists to be made, as if writing items in neat vertical rows might stave off randomness and chaos. I had a pile of student work to read, not to mention the usual chores before leaving home: bills to be paid, the refrigerator to be cleaned out, our dogs to be taken to the kennel. I reveled in the normalcy, but as I went through the motions, within me a pendulum contin-ued to swing back and forth. On one side was Ben Walden—the fact of him, of his existence in the world. And on the other side was the tangled story of my parents and my continued, fervent desire to believe that they hadn't betrayed me.

I tried with varying degrees of success to push thoughts of Ben to the side, and to trust Michael's certainty that more would be revealed. I wrote my imaginary responses. And I con-tinued to read books about the practice and history of donor insemination, searching for clues, as if there might be a case study in which I would recognize my parents and all would be revealed. I combed the Internet for mentions of Edmond Farris, and finally I stumbled on a lead. A graduate student who was helping me with research was given the name of a doctor who had begun his career at Penn and remembered the Farris Institute.

A few days before our trip to Provincetown, I made a phone date with Dr. Alan DeCherney. I was in New York that afternoon for meetings and didn't want to speak to the elderly doctor from a noisy street corner or restaurant. I got in touch with a friend, a boutique owner, and asked if I could hole myself up in the back room of her shop for an hour. Surrounded by racks of jackets and piles of designer jeans, I opened my notebook and dialed DeCherney.

After I introduced myself, and explained the nature of my interest in Edmond Farris and the Farris Institute, there was a brief pause on the other end of the phone.

"It's unbelievable that you found me," he finally said. "I'm probably the only person alive who can tell you about Farris."

He proceeded to provide me with some background. From 1970 to 1974 DeCherney had been a medical resident at Penn, where the strong suit in ob-gyn was infertility. A friend of his who ran the chemistry lab had lost a toddler in a tragic accident, and he and his wife were desperate to get pregnant again but had been unable to conceive until they found Edmond Farris.

"Were lots of people at Penn aware of Farris?" I asked DeCherney.

"I never knew a doctor who knew him, nor a patient who knew him," he responded. "He was off in his own little clinic."

As I pondered how this could have been possible, DeCherney added a detail.

"Farris was an outlaw," he said. "He was practicing medicine without a license."

My mother in the car, the darkness, the inky black of the Hudson River, the graceful arc of lights illuminating the George Washington Bridge. *Institute. Philadelphia. Your father. Slow sperm. Brilliant doctor.* How did I know to commit her words to memory? *Not a pretty story.*

So Farris had been no brand name. My parents had gone to a back-alley rogue scientist who threw out the rulebook and got the job done. My parents were law-abiding people. What Farris was doing was lawless. How desperate must they have been as they made those trips to Philadelphia?

"Farris had a gimmick," DeCherney went on. "He had a way of measuring LH so he could tell when women were ovulating. The gimmick he had wasn't fraudulent—he was onto something."

I thought of the story the endocrinologist Leonard Hayflick had told me about the white rats being injected with the urine of hopeful women. This was Farris's gimmick. "The chemistry part was real," DeCherney went on. "Years later—in 1976—it became common practice to use the LH test to time ovulation."

How could Farris have established his own clinic on the campus of Penn when he wasn't an M.D.? How did he advertise in the medical school for donors? He pioneered a fertility test that in time became the gold standard, for which he never got the credit. Why was he now no more than a footnote in the history of reproductive medicine in this country? But what rose to the top of all those questions was only this: what happened once my parents had committed to Farris's back-alley operation? What would he have told them? Was it possible that DeCherney could shed any light on an intimate conversation at which he wasn't present?

"What I'm most interested in," I said, "is what my parents knew."

"Well, they certainly would have mixed your father's sperm with donor sperm," he responded matter-of-factly. "This was the practice."

"And they—my parents—would have been told it was happening?"

My friend's tiny toy poodle skittered into the back room.

"In a way. Yes and no."

"What do you mean? What language would have been used? What words?" I was talking fast now, rushing, impatient. Yes and no? I couldn't live with yes and no.

"Your parents would have been told it was a treatment."

A treatment.

Everything slowed down. Such an innocuous word. A gentle word. A *medical* word. A word that could mean absolutely anything.

"A treatment for your father's low sperm count," DeCherney continued. "They would have been told that the treatment would help the husband's sperm."

Alone in the dim back room, I felt something new. I closed my eyes and saw my hopeful parents sitting across the desk from Edmond Farris—after three, four, five inseminations with only my father's sperm, after three, four miscarriages. Time was running out. *Pru u'rvu*. My educated parents, who knew something about biology, making a dark and complicated decision to hear only what they wanted to hear, and to believe only what they longed to believe.

"By the time I finished my training, in the mid-1970s," DeCherney said, "it was considered passé."

"What was considered passé?" I asked. "The mixing of sperm? Calling it a treatment?"

"All of it," DeCherney replied. "They eventually stopped mixing sperm because it didn't help, and it gave people a false sense of security. I thought it was okay though," he added.

"Why?" I asked. "Why did you think it was okay?"

"I mean, it all worked out. Your father never knew."

There it was. Four little words. *Your father never knew.*

I tried to take a deep breath.

"There always would have been a question mark," DeCherney said. "That was the whole point. To protect the father."

"But what about protecting the child?" I asked. "I mean, it didn't entirely work out. Because now *I* know."

"Precisely," DeCherney said. He sounded almost rueful. "Now there are no more secrets."

34

Ben had mentioned his children in most of his correspondence with me. It was clear that he had shared the outlines of the situation. There it was again, that word: *situation*. Had he told them my name? He seemed to be trying to control things. If he had shared my name, then my half siblings would be able to look me up. They could get in touch with me. They could do their own genetic testing, if they so desired. I had no way of knowing what was going on, on the other side of the country. But what I could do was continue to gather information, which allowed me to feel some semblance of control as well.

I had a half sister and two half brothers. I had spent fifty-four years thinking Susie was my half sister, so the idea of a sister wasn't foreign to me. But the concept of a half brother was new territory. Both half brothers were married with a couple of kids. I had already ascertained that one was an attorney, and the other worked in the tech industry. I found my half sister on Facebook and Twitter. There we both floated, digital ghosts, our two avatars among millions of avatars populating a universe made of pixels and bits that connected me to the

Waldens, the Waldens to me—enabling not only the swiftness of discovery but discovery itself.

Emily Walden had inherited her Brazilian mother's jet-black hair and dark eyes, but still I could see the resemblance between us. We had the same high forehead, the same proportion to our features. The details available about Emily made me think that we might easily be friends. Certainly we had a lot in common. We both had graduated from women's colleges. Her politics were liberal. She worked for a philanthropic foundation. On Twitter, she followed many of the same people I did. Though she wasn't particularly active on social media, it was still possible to paint a picture, however faint, of her life. She was married and had two kids, a girl and a boy. The boy looked to be the same age as Jacob.

Michael was able to track traffic on my website and had statistics that told him how many people were on my website at any given time, how long they lingered on certain pages, and where they were from. In the weeks following Ben's final communication, there was an unusual spike of visitors from Portland, Oregon. Was it a coincidence that several of them spent hours reading deep into my old essays and interviews—particularly those that related to family? Or that quite a few people went back to the beginning of my decade-old blog to read every post? At times I thought maybe we were imagining things. Maybe I just had some dedicated readers in Portland. But at other times I envisioned us—Ben's family and mine—all of us reading, searching, digging toward some sense of one another, and of this unexpected turn our lives had taken. Perhaps as I was watching YouTube videos of Santa and grandchildren's excursions to SeaWorld, they were reading essays about my father's time with the Lubavitcher Rebbe, or my spiritual journey away from my strict religious upbringing.

We were packing up the car for our trip to Provincetown when I heard the sound of Michael's feet on the stairs. It was the sound of news. I was storing my power cords and computer in their carrying bag when he stepped into my office, open laptop in hand. He didn't look stricken the way he had at the beginning of the summer, his screen displaying the DNA results that would change my life. This time he looked triumphant.

"Emily just followed you on Twitter," he said.

He showed me her name atop a list of my newest followers.

Emily Walden. There she was. I felt a strange and instant comfort. She did know about me. She did. And she was reaching out.

The three of us piled into our packed-to-the-gills car and began the long drive to Provincetown. I kept my phone in my lap, refreshing Twitter again and again to see if perhaps Emily Walden had thought better of it and unfollowed me. But there she continued to be. My thumb hovered over her avatar, a Bitmoji of a dark-haired, apple-cheeked woman.

It took two days for me to follow her back. I was afraid of seeming too jumpy, too eager—though of course I was both. Finally, early one morning, as I sat in the sun-drenched kitchen of our cottage at the arts center, I touched *follow* on my phone's screen. I saw it—a vision—two half sisters who had never known of one another's existence, sending the most modern version of a smoke signal, each from her own coast.

I see you.

I see you, too.

35

Later, I will become a student of trauma. I will read deeply on the subject as a way of understanding the two opposite poles of my own history: the trauma my parents must have experienced in order to have made a decision so painful that it was buried at the moment it was made, and the trauma of my discovery of that decision more than half a century later.

Anything was capable of setting it off. A guest at a party in my home admired the sepia photograph of the small boy in his bowler hat. *Who's that?* The answer I had always given was no longer true. Or a doctor's appointment at which I was asked to update my medical history. How could I explain that my father was no longer deceased? While having my vision checked, I let my longtime ophthalmologist know that I am genetically predisposed to a rare eye condition. *Nothing to worry about,* Ben had said. *It would be reasonable to be followed.*

It is the nature of trauma that, when left untreated, it deepens over time. I had experienced trauma over the years and had developed ways of dealing with it. I meditated each morning. I had a decades-long yoga practice. I had suffered other traumas—my parents' car accident, Jacob's childhood illness—and had come out the other side, eventually. What I didn't understand was that as terrible as these were, they were singular incidents. The car crash. The diagnosis. In the aftermath, what was left to be dealt with was the grief, the anxiety. But this—the discovery that I wasn't who I had believed myself to be all my life, that my parents had on some level, no matter how subtle, made the choice to keep the truth of my identity from me—this was no singular incident. It wasn't something outside myself, to be held to the light and examined, and finally understood. It was inseparable from myself. It *was* myself.

The boa constrictor had begun to metabolize the elephant. I began to visualize my parents' choices on a continuum, like weights on a scale. On one end, there was absolute lack of knowledge. But my desperate parents, struggling to have a child, had gone to a lawless institute near the campus of Penn to see a mad scientist known specifically for donor insemination. Increasingly, absolute lack of knowledge had begun to seem like my own self-protective fantasy.

Everyone seemed to be telling me that my parents had possessed some level of knowledge. Wendy Kramer, Leonard Hayflick, Alan DeCherney, Rabbi Lookstein, Aunt Shirley—all of them had gently or not so gently let me know that there was agency. My parents had made a decision. And no matter how difficult or painful, I had to open the door to the likelihood that they had some awareness. The weights inched further over to conscious knowledge with each passing week.

Their trauma became mine—had always been mine. It was my inheritance, my lot. My parents' tortured pact of secrecy was as much a part of me as the genes that had been passed down by my mother and Ben Walden. It was another facet of the whole picture. It felt as if I had only ever been able to see in two dimensions, and now I had been handed a pair of 3-D glasses. The clarity was both liberating and devastating. I listened over and over again to the interview with the psychiatrist Bessel van der Kolk which I had noted on that early index card: "The nature of trauma," van der Kolk had said, "is that you have no recollection of it as a story. The nature of traumatic experience is that the brain doesn't allow a story to be created."

I grew up to become a storyteller. I moved from fiction to memoir, writing one, two, three, four—now five—memoirs. I captured my life, and the life of my family, between the pages of book after book and thought: *There, that's it. Now I understand.* I dug until my shovel hit rock. Sometimes people suggested that I must have an amazing memory—that surely I must recall so many scenes, moments, sensory details from my early years. But the truth is that I have a terrible memory. I struggled to access any of my childhood or even my teenage years. I had no recollection of it as a story. And so I followed my own line of words to see where it would lead me. I understood that there were layers, striations of consciousness, inaccessible through analysis or intellect. Only in a state of half dreaming could I begin—and then only barely—to touch the truth.

I am the black box, discovered years—many years—after the crash. The pilots, the crew, the passengers have long been committed to the sea. Nothing is left of them. Fathoms deep, I have spent my life transmitting the faintest signal. *Over here! Over here!* I have settled upon the ocean floor. I am also the diver who has discovered the black box. What's this? I had been looking for it all my life without knowing it existed. Now I hold it in my hands. It may or may not contain clues. It is a witness to a history it recorded but did not see. What went on in that plane? Why did it fall from the sky?

36

Our week in Provincetown, usually a fun time for my family, was instead a struggle. Each morning I met with my class around a workshop table in a high-ceilinged studio to discuss their stories. The subject matter—as is often the case in a creative nonfiction class—was thorny and painful: addiction, suicide, grief, estrangement, abuse. The difficult passages of people's lives and the desire to wrest meaning from those passages never fail to move me. As a teacher, I am accustomed to being able to hold my students' stories with both rigor and care. I am usually able to leave myself and my own troubles behind when I teach. But during this particular week I felt unsteady.

In a journal I had kept in my early twenties, I berated myself, just a short while after my father had died, for still being in the thick of grief. As a grown woman, stumbling across that journal entry, I wanted to reach back and let that young, lost girl know it was okay. I wanted to tell her that grief—particularly the phenomenon known as complicated grief—runs its own course in its own time. But it was hard for me to allow myself that same compassion now. I tried to tuck my sorrow away each day as I taught, went to the beach, biked around town, ate lobster rolls on Commercial Street with Michael and Jacob—but when I awoke each morning it was to the wallop of shock and the remembering all over again as if for the first time.

All the while, as I began to reassemble and re-understand the childhood I could hardly remember, Ben Walden was never far from my mind. Friends kept sending me articles about donor-conceived people discovering half siblings or searching for biological fathers. I wondered if Ben was also reading and thinking about any of this—or whether he had moved on. Was he at all tortured by the idea that he had a biological child—or likely multiple biological children—wandering the earth? That his actions had living consequences? I also wondered if his daughter knew that he had written me a letter severing our communication. Would Emily have told him that she followed me on Twitter? Was the Walden family sitting around the dinner table discussing the matter of me?

Finally, sunburned, sticky, tired, our skin salty, sand covering the floor of our car, we began our trek home. I closed my eyes as Michael navigated vacation traffic; I was exhausted from my week of making room for other people's stories when I hardly had the space for my own. In the years we'd been coming to Provincetown, we'd established a routine to break up the long, monotonous ride. We stopped at a roadside tourist attraction, Arnold's Lobster & Clam Bar, and gorged on towering trays of fried clams and onion rings, washed down with cold soda.

This annual trip spelled end-of-summer for our family. Jacob would be getting ready to start his junior year of high school. Michael and I, too, were in back-to-school mode—I was busy with plans for my upcoming book, and Michael was in the throes of putting together a new film. We had plenty going on—but no matter what was happening in our daily lives, my mind continued to leap back to only one story, and it seemed like it would be that way forever.

We had stopped for gas somewhere along the Mid-Cape Highway when I dug into my purse for my phone and saw, amid announcements of sales and political entreaties, Ben Walden's name. His subject line read: *Second thoughts.*

I said nothing. Jacob was in the backseat, listening to music on his headphones. Michael was inside the rest stop. I spent a long moment looking at the subject of the email before I opened it. *Second thoughts.*

Dear Dani,
My wife, Pilar, and I will be flying to Newark on Monday October 10 and will be in Paramus for a few days in order to be with an ill friend. We'll then be driving to Philadelphia for a class reunion and to visit my sister there.

I have been having second thoughts about meeting with you. It may well be the right thing for both of us to bring more of a sense of reality to our human connection. I know your schedule is busy, but would it be possible to meet with us for lunch somewhere within a twenty-minute drive from Paramus? Either Tuesday the eleventh or Wednesday the twelfth would work. Or, if you happen to be in the Philadelphia area, we could work something out later in the week.

I apologize for wavering on the idea of meeting.

I hope that you are still interested and that the timing works. Your husband, of course, is more than welcome to join us.

Best regards,
Ben

37

From the time I was a child, I thought of the month of September also as the month of Elul, the last month of the Jewish calendar, leading to the High Holy Days. Elul is meant to be a period of reckoning with oneself in preparation for Rosh Hashanah, when God opens the Book of Life and judges each one of us. How have we sinned? How might we repent? Following Elul are the Days of Awe, the ten-day stretch between Rosh Hashanah and Yom Kippur, a period of intense transformation fraught with meaning and dread. On Erev Yom Kippur, God gathers the great court to determine our fate, and on Yom Kippur, the Book of Life is sealed for the coming year. In synagogue, we list our sins, pounding our chests above our hearts: *For the sin we have committed before You by false denial and lying. For the sin we have committed before You by a confused heart.*

Some of my clearest memories of my father are of praying with him. As a young girl, I was allowed to sit next to him in *shul,* and I could feel the way his body relaxed when he davened, the way his voice became stronger and fuller within the plaintive melodies of the Hebrew liturgy. The synagogue was his home. When he shook his *tallis* from its velvet pouch and wrapped it around his shoulders, he became larger, almost mystical. Here in *shul,* prayer was our secret language, our way of connecting. We had the choreography down. We knew just what to do. Here we stand. Here we sit. Here we sway. Here we close our *siddurs.* Here we sing *Ein Keloheinu.* Here we kiss each other's cheeks and say: *Good Shabbos.* What thoughts ran through my father's mind as he listed those sins, his little girl beside him? Was he confused? Did he feel he had lied?

It was a solemn undertaking, this business of reckoning. The Sunday before Rosh Hashanah, my father would make the trip from our home in New Jersey to the cemetery in Brooklyn where his father and grandparents were buried. He never asked my mother or me to accompany him on this journey. I can see him now: he parks his car near the small utility building just inside the gates, then walks along the narrow paths of the vast graveyard, thousands upon thousands of headstones etched in Hebrew spread out in every direction until he arrives at the Shapiro family plot. In the distance, the rumble of an elevated train and the white noise of traffic on the Belt Parkway. A wild dog barks. He unlatches the heavy chain that cordons the family plot off from the path. Perhaps he sits on a bench for a few moments and thinks of his father. He recites the Mourner's Kaddish at the foot of his father's grave. *Yit'gadal v'yit'kadash sh'mei raba.* He pokes around the roots and pebbles, the fallen leaves, until he finds just the right handful of stones. He places one atop each of his ancestors' graves, a custom that symbolizes permanence. Does my father foresee his own early death—only a decade away? He can't envision the future: his daughter making her way alone down the cemetery's narrow paths, year after year, reciting the Mourner's Kaddish for him, warming a stone in her hands.

The dates Ben proposed in early October most likely fell within Elul. Before I had a chance to even glance at my calendar, Michael had finished gassing up the car and climbed back into the driver's seat. I wordlessly handed him my phone. *Ben Walden.* The feeling—the predominant one—was of being flooded with relief. *See? I wasn't wrong about him.* A hard knot inside me unraveled. I had the strangest sense that I knew him, though I had never spent a moment in his presence; his last letter to me had seemed harsh, perhaps influenced by others, and didn't feel expressive of his true self. But how could I possibly know anything about Ben Walden's true self? Did the genetic code that linked us allow me to recognize him? Was there a gene for depth of thought? For kindness? *It may well be the right thing for both of us.* Not just for me. For him as well. *Sense of reality to our human connection.* In the weeks of silence between us, I had become real to him. *Apologize for wavering. Hope that you are still interested.*

"I told you something would happen," Michael said. He reached over and squeezed my hand.

"Yeah, but *this.*" I stared at the screen. Lunch. New Jersey. October. I studied Ben's email as if it were a cryptogram. I noticed that he misspelled the word *thoughts* in the subject line: *Second thoughtus.*

As Michael pulled back onto the highway, I opened the calendar on my phone and looked up the two dates Ben had proposed. They didn't fall over Elul. They fell on Erev Yom Kippur and Yom Kippur—the holiest days of the year.

Dear Ben,

I would be happy to meet you and Pilar on Tuesday, October 11, near Paramus. I'm glad you reconsidered. My husband, Michael, will join us, too. If you'd like, I can find a quiet restaurant within twenty minutes of Paramus—I know the area somewhat.

Thanks for getting back in touch. I look forward to meeting you.

My best,

Dani

I had become a master of restraint and understatement. Our lunch was six weeks away. I wrote the date—*lunch with Ben*—in my calendar. It gave me a jolt each time I noticed it, a stark, otherwise blank page amid all the others: *Brattleboro Festival, reading at Southampton College, haircut, teaching at Kripalu, dinner with the Campbells, Jacob PSATs. Lunch with Ben.*

The six weeks leading up to our meeting were all preamble. I could think of little else. Each time I wrote Ben, I read Michael the email before I sent it. What if he got cold feet again? What if he changed his mind? What if he became ill? Our delicate back-and-forth continued, though the tone of his emails was markedly warmer. Something had fallen away from him—a tremulous, suspicious sense of me as other. He easily shared personal details: he wasn't really familiar with New Jersey, though he had worked in Trenton the summer before medical school. He preferred Italian food to Greek. He was feeling very well, thank you, other than the usual aches and pains of aging. He sent me his mobile number in case we needed to text each other on the day. And then he wrote two brief lines that for the first time made me weep. *Strange how I misspelled thoughts as "thoughtus." Perhaps it was an appropriate slip.*

38

What do we inherit, and how, and why? The relatively new field of epigenetics studies the impact of environment and experience on genes themselves. How much had the gene pool of the Waldens—that apparently cheerful extended family I had seen singing on YouTube—formed me? I did not come from the line of small, wiry, dark-eyed people of the shtetl, the men swaying over crumbling tombstones, prayer books in their hands. The imprint of pogroms, of the difficulties and sorrows of immigrant life was not mine—at least not in a physical sense. But I had carried these things a long way in my heart. I was of that dusty and doomed Polish village—and I was not. What had I inherited psychologically? What was in my blood? I was made of three people: my mother, my father, Ben Walden. Disparate worlds had been floating and colliding within me all my life.

To contend with these invisible floating worlds, I had created a narrative edifice, I now understood. Story after story kept me from ever inching too close to the truth. People had told me every single day of my life that I didn't look like I belonged in my family—nor did I feel I belonged in my family—yet I didn't stop to consider what this might mean. I couldn't afford to. Not even after I learned the method of my conception at the age of twenty-five. Not even after Susie told me I ought to look into it.

The clues screamed in neon. But I could not see them. After all, plenty of people feel or look "other" than their parents or siblings. Biology doesn't promise similarity. Traits skip generations. Characteristics emerge, seemingly out of nowhere. Our parents seem alien to us. My mother, certainly, had always seemed alien to me, biology be damned. And so I built my narrative edifice, brick by brick: my mother was a pathological narcissist who had a borderline personality disorder; my father was depressed, shattered by marital misfortune; I was an Orthodox Jewish girl who looked like she could have gotten bread from the Nazis; I was the hard-won only child of my older parents. My sense of otherness derived from these—and only these—facts.

Ben Walden looked at his own simple typo and saw a Freudian slip, potential meaning. He didn't have second thoughts but second thoughts about *us*—he and I. *Thoughtus.* I had noticed the typo, too, of course, and had smiled at it. It had the kind of psychological nuance I tend to enjoy. The feeling I would have again and again, of recognizing myself in Ben, was one I could become aware of only as I realized I had never experienced it before.

I had not seen myself in my father. Nor had I seen myself reflected back in my mother, no matter that she had given birth to me. Nor had I felt a kinship with Susie, as much as I tried. A friend who had once met Susie later told me she had always known we couldn't possibly be related. It wasn't only a physical thing. It was a disjunction of the spirit. We didn't fit. We didn't—any of us—belong together.

As the weeks ticked closer toward my meeting with Ben, I wondered if he, too, felt this strange sense of familiarity. How much of my work had he read? My books and essays would have given him a smattering of insights and clues. But I had a powerful instinct about him—the kind that doesn't come from study. His gentleness, his manner, his way of being, signaled something deeper.

I tried to read as much as I could about what it must have been like to have been him—a medical student, a sperm donor—in the early 1960s. I wanted to put myself in his place. He had walked through the doors of that institute in Philadelphia with its cages of albino rats. He had been there. Quite often, by his own admission. I couldn't see talking with him about it—and yet I couldn't see not talking with him about it. I found images of the nine-story Art Deco building on the corner of South Thirty-sixth Street, central to Penn's campus, which now houses the women's clothing store Loft. The Farris Institute had been on the sixth floor. I thought of my parents, side by side in the elevator, riding up. And of Ben Walden, stepping into the same elevator, moments later.

The research continued to be bizarre and almost unbearable. I discovered an obituary of Edmond Farris that made no sense—he had died suddenly, of a heart attack, several months before I was conceived. If Farris was dead, then who was running his institute? A man I met on Wendy Kramer's Donor Sibling Registry told me that Augusta Farris—not a doctor, not a scientist, in fact a cookbook illustrator—had put on a white lab coat and continued her husband's work after his unexpected death. Did I owe my existence to Augusta Farris? This new information left me reeling. What potent combination of lawlessness, secrecy, desire, shame, greed, and confusion had led to my conception? Would Ben Walden have known anything about the inner workings of Farris, or had he simply slipped through the back door, performed his services, then headed blithely back to Chemistry Lab?

A hardcover book arrived in the mail during that mystifying month of Elul—one I had ordered from a used-book store online months earlier. It was titled simply *Artificial Insemination*. Its spine cracked when I opened it, emitting the musty scent of old, abandoned paper. The book was nearly as old as I was. Its author, Dr. Wilfred Finegold, had been the head of the Department of Sterility at Planned Parenthood in Pittsburgh. Leafing through chapters like "Artificial Insemination and Animal Husbandry" and "Anticipated Legal Problems," I turned to one called "The Couple—The Donor." Finegold offered a list of standards all vigilant sterologists—and presumably a widowed cookbook illustrator in a white lab coat—should follow in order to select donors who would produce the highest-quality semen for their patients:

1. The donor must remain an unknown.
2. The donor should be in fine health mentally and physically.
3. The donor should be of fine physical stock.
4. The donor should be of high fertility.
5. The donor should be of excellent character.
6. The donor must be cooperative.
7. The donor's characteristics must match those of the patient's husband.
8. The donors should be men of science or medicine.
9. Multiple donors should be utilized if possible.

The chapter concludes: "It isn't absurd to presume that a child of artificial insemination has an advantage eugenically, mentally and physically. The donors chosen are devoid of hereditary taints; they have the mental capacity to advance to upper classes in schools of medicine; they are physically able to procreate and they are even free of such irritating conditions as hay fever or allergy."

39

My shoulder had begun to ache over the summer, and by early autumn I could hardly move it. It became impossible to reach for a dish on a high shelf, or even strap on my seat belt. If the body can be seen as a metaphor, then it seemed I was shouldering something, carrying a giant boulder on my back all through the night in my sleep, then awakening to a half-frozen self. Nothing helped. Not physical therapy, not yoga, not even a cortisone shot.

Days before lunch with Ben, I got the name of an acupuncturist in the Berkshires, an hour's drive from my house. I hoped that he might help release me from whatever had me in its grip. Driving was good. Driving was a moving meditation for me, as I sped along winding country roads trying not to think—reasoning got me nowhere. I had reread some of my early books in recent weeks and was taken aback, again and again, at the choices I'd made, the language I'd used—particularly in my fiction—that pointed to some sort of consciousness lurking just beyond my ability to perceive it. The truth had been inside me all along.

In my first, highly autobiographical novel, the narrator is aware that she is out of place in her father's Orthodox Jewish family and longs to be a part of them. But she is haunted by the fact that no one ever recognizes her as part of the family by her face. In a much later novel, a secret wears away at a family until it is very nearly destroyed; parents with the best of intentions make selfish decisions affecting the fate of their child. What had I known without knowing? My unconscious mind had shaped stories out of its own rough landscape. I had scrambled from one rocky path to the next. I had spent all my life writing my way through darkness like a miner in a cave until I spit into a plastic vial and the lights blinked on.

After the acupuncturist took a long history—and I haltingly answered the question of whether my father was living or dead—he asked me to lie faceup on a narrow table. He placed needles along the tops of my shoulders, the insides of my wrists, my calves, ankles, and at the center of my sternum. He covered me lightly with a blanket and started to leave me alone in the small room, but before he did, he stopped.

"Do you know the three great spiritual questions?" he asked.

My eyes were closed, stinging from my disclosure, as they often did.

"Who am I?" I whispered and paused. I couldn't remember the other two.

We were silent for a long moment. Outside his office, on the main street of Stockbridge, I could hear the whoosh of a passing car, the chirp of a lone bird.

Finally, he continued. "Why am I here?"

Tears ran down my temples and into my hair.

He paused before offering me the last question.

"And how shall I live?"

. . .

I lay on that table for what seemed like hours. Hanging on the wall next to me were several Eastern medicine diagrams of the human body. They looked like intricate topographical maps, with well over three hundred individual points lining the main meridians. Lungs, large intestine, stomach, spleen. Heart, small intestine, bladder, kidneys. Pericardium, gallbladder, liver. Fine lines and arrows dipped and swirled in elaborate patterns and channels that I found at once disconcerting and comforting. How had I lived my life without being able to answer that first and most fundamental of all questions: *Who am I?* Without an answer, how could I possibly have fully moved on to the others? *Why am I here?* Augusta Farris in her white lab coat, my parents in all their shame and desire, Ben Walden and his assurances of anonymity. Shirley's words floated back to me: *not an accident of history.* This was the challenge that had been set down at my feet. *How shall I live?*

40

The streets of Teaneck, New Jersey, were nearly deserted on Erev Yom Kippur. We had arrived early and circled the block a couple of times to get our bearings. In the emptiness and quiet—not typical of an ordinary weekday—I could sense the town's anticipation of the holiest day in the Jewish year. We passed a large synagogue, one of several. By this evening it would be crowded with congregants, and the sound of the *shofar* would pierce the air. A suburb of New York City, Teaneck has long been known for its tight-knit Jewish population. My father's younger brother raised his family in this town, and I counted at least two cousins among its many rabbis. This only added to the surreal nature of the moment. Of all the possible destinations, this place to which I felt an uneasy connection had turned out to be the best meeting spot for lunch with Ben and Pilar.

Michael and I parked just outside Amarone, an Italian restaurant I had chosen. *I know the area somewhat.* In fact, I knew the area not at all and had relied on the recommendations of local friends, one of whom had even scouted a couple of places and sent me photographs. Much of my anxiety had been poured into making a restaurant choice. It needed to be quiet but not too quiet. Not empty at the lunch hour, or too busy—I didn't want us to feel rushed. Oh, and not too expensive, but nice enough to be relaxing. I then called the restaurant and asked for a corner table—my friend had specified which one—and explained that it was a special occasion. No, not a birthday or an anniversary, nothing like that. Just important.

I was in a state of high alert. Even after all the careful planning, it seemed crazy and impossible, as if I had been swept into someone's novel—someone's melodramatic novel—and I was playing a character rather than living my life. And then there were the practical concerns: Was I going to risk alienating him by asking questions about what he remembered from that time? Were we going to keep it at polite chitchat? How much would we share with each other? And what about his wife? I wondered what it could possibly be like—married for fifty years, retired, with three grown children—to discover that your husband had another child. From what I could gather about Pilar from bits and pieces available online, she seemed to have lived a traditional life for a woman of her generation. She was a doctor's wife. An avid golfer. She and Ben were dedicated congregants of a local church. My news must have rocked their world—and yet they had come around to deciding to have this meeting. *Second thoughtus.*

"We should go in," Michael said.

We still had half an hour. Maybe they had arrived early as well. What if they were already inside? I wanted to stay suspended in this moment of before. I didn't have the muscles for this. How could I be emotionally or psychologically equipped to meet the biological father I hadn't ever known existed? It was as if I had just strapped on my ice skates and was expected to perform a triple axel.

"I'm not ready."

We sat in the car watching the entrance of Amarone. The restaurant's maroon canopy hung over a small patio dotted with tables. It was still quite warm, unseasonably so. I had worn a favorite sweater over a silk camisole and corduroy jeans for my meeting with my biological father. *Father,* Michael had said that morning as he was getting dressed. *We've been married twenty years, and I'm about to meet your father.*

I had considered wearing something of my dad's to keep him close to me. But I didn't want him at the table with Ben. I didn't want him hovering there, stricken, sorrowful. It felt like a betrayal of one father, that I was meeting my other father. And if my dad *had* known—had always loved me, as I knew he did, in full recognition that I wasn't his biological child—then that, too, would make this day fraught beyond measure. If he had chosen to keep such a massive secret, how could it feel to have that secret revealed now, when it was too late to discuss or make amends? I once heard a psychic say that the dead are able to observe the living with compassion but not emotion. In that case, the entire restaurant would be filled with my long-lost relatives: mother, father, aunts, uncles, floating, invisible, impassively witnessing the meeting about to take place.

I watched the sidewalk and front door of Amarone.

"Let's go in," Michael said again.

"I can't." I felt pinned to the spot. "How do I greet him? Do I hug him? Shake his hand?"

"You'll know."

"And who should pick up the check?"

"We'll pick up the check."

"You don't think that will insult him?"

"Honey, you're going to have to let this play out."

Just then—seeing before I fully registered what I was seeing—I caught a glimpse of an older couple slowly walking up the sidewalk in the near distance. The man was tall, white-haired, wearing a blue button-down shirt and khakis. He held the bent elbow of a petite, elegant woman. It was Ben.

"Get out of the car," Michael said.

"I can't. Let's wait."

"Get out of the car," he repeated. "Now." He said it lovingly but firmly, not taking no for an answer, as if teaching a child to swim or ride a bike. This was my moment to flail or to fall on my own. I opened the car door. I saw them seeing me. There was no going back.

The four of us moved toward one another. It was probably no more than half a dozen steps. What now? There seemed to be nothing to do but acknowledge the strangeness, to live inside the world of it.

"Ben," I said. "Hello."

It was bewildering to look at him—to see my features reflected back at me. All those staring contests I'd held with myself as a child were about this, I now understood. I had been searching and searching for the truth in the mirror, trying to make sense of my own face. Here it was, finally, irrefutably, in the form of the old man standing before me.

I stuck out my hand. "I'm Dani."

His eyes crinkled as he smiled. Both of us were flushed bright pink. Michael and Pilar were now both standing slightly apart from us. A passerby might take us for a family.

Ben took an awkward half step toward me. His voice was like a fragment from a remembered dream. His first words:

"Would it be all right to give you a hug?"

41

We were seated, as I had requested, at a secluded corner table. Checked tablecloth, leather menus, Italian bread, a small pitcher of olive oil. Our water glasses filled and filled again. We didn't touch our menus for at least the first hour. Beneath the table, I couldn't stop shaking. I had no appetite. I directed most of my conversation to Pilar, but my ears were trained on Ben's conversation with Michael. They were talking of simple things, ordinary things. Both men had been in the Peace Corps. They had done some research on each other—they knew they had that in common. Ben and Pilar had read three of my books and were in the middle of a book Michael had written about foreign aid. We had all boned up, as if for an important exam. But there was something I had promised myself I would say, and I said it as soon as I had an opening to cut through the polite chitchat.

"I want to thank you," I addressed Ben. "You didn't have to do this. When I first wrote you, you could have ignored it."

His cheeks became even redder.

"He deleted it from his mailbox the second he read it," Pilar said. She had a lilting voice and retained her Brazilian accent. "Like a hot potato!"

Those interminable, surreal days in San Francisco. Checking my email, obsessively checking. Envisioning the doctor in Portland opening my letter. He had deleted it. He had hoped it would just go away.

"Then you wrote me again," Ben said. "And I fished it out of my trash."

"I was shocked!" Pilar's voice rose. It will be months before I know what she really said to Ben: *How could you have been so stupid?*

"It just never occurred to me that I might have biological children out there," he said. "I donated for a short while. I honestly never thought about it after I finished medical school."

Michael and I exchanged a quick glance. It seemed purposeful, Ben's phrase. He was letting us know that he hadn't been prolific. That I was not in a situation—like some I had read about—where I might have hundreds of half siblings. Which of course was the very scenario about which he and Pilar must have been most terrified.

In time, I will question how it could be possible that Ben—a man of medicine, who specialized in medical ethics—had never considered that he might have biological children. I will think of the three of them—my mother, my father, Ben Walden—all burying the consequences of their actions so deep that it seemed there weren't any consequences at all. But not on this day. On this day my entire being was trying to absorb as much as possible. Who knew if we would ever be together again?

As we finally ordered lunch—Caprese salad, grilled chicken—we went over the whole story detail by detail. The way Michael zeroed in on the Farris Institute. Our hunch about the donor being a medical student at Penn. The appearance of Adam Thomas on my Ancestry page. The ease with which we found him—Ben's nephew, my first cousin—on Facebook. Ben's sister's obituary. In the absence of A.T. we would not have been gathered at that table. The elderly doctor from Portland and I would have remained oblivious and anonymous to one another. I would have discovered that I wasn't my dad's biological daughter but known nothing more. I might have spent the rest of my life looking into the faces of certain men, wondering how I came to be.

Pilar was telling me about her golf game, their lives in a retirement community near Portland, and stories of their three children, but I continued to have one ear tuned in to Ben and Michael's conversation. I heard Ben ask if Michael had seen a photo of his daughter, Emily. I could feel Ben's gaze upon me—his astonishment at the resemblance. Every cell in my body was on high alert. I had questions for him I felt I couldn't ask. I didn't dare upset the delicate balance. We were four people who genuinely liked one another. We had entire conversations in which the reason for being together seemed to be momentarily forgotten—that is, except by me.

I kept looking over at Ben and then away. *Father*. He didn't feel like my father. He hadn't raised me. We'd met hours earlier. So who was he to me—and I to him? *Biological. Social.* Later, it will occur to me that Ben Walden felt, to me, like my native country. I had never lived in this country. I had never spoken its language or become steeped in its customs. I had no passport or record of citizenship. Still, I had been shaped by my country of origin all my life, suffused with an inchoate longing to know my own land.

·   ·   ·

The sunlight that had streamed through the restaurant's windows had now vanished. Four and a half hours had passed in a moment. The other diners had long since vacated their tables. The waitstaff was setting up the restaurant for dinner all around us. Dusk would soon fall—my relatives would be preparing for *yontef*. Pilar asked to see a photo of Jacob, and I scrolled through albums on my phone for the one I had planned to show them, if asked. It had been taken over the summer; Jacob's hair was bleached by the sun and he was tanned from months outside, shooting films and playing tennis. He looked like a golden boy. He looked quite a bit like Ben. Pilar inhaled sharply when she saw him. *So handsome.* Then she passed my phone to Ben.

At some point Ben seemed to have made a decision to trust me—to put aside his concerns about privacy, or my being a writer, or worries about possible other offspring. Perhaps this had happened before we even met. The week prior, on Rosh Hashanah, he had sent me a note wishing us *L'shana tova tikateivu.* May you be inscribed in the Book of Life for a good year. He must have looked it up. He was reaching out a hand, respecting our differences while understanding the enormity of our bond.

After he studied the photo of Jacob for a good long minute, Ben picked up his own phone and handed it to me. It was open to a folder of photographs. He cleared his throat.

"I put these together, thinking I might show them to you," he said. "Ancestors. Family."

A man and woman stood on the porch of a farmhouse. She wore a flowered dress. He was in shirtsleeves. I once again had the sensation of not being able to compute what I was looking at.

"My parents," said Ben. "At home in Ohio."

Grandparents. Not the imposing bald man with the yarmulke and pince-nez. Not the regal woman in the gilded frame, hair pulled tightly back, a brooch at her throat. Those were the grandparents of my psyche but not of my being. I was descended from this couple. I searched their faces as if I might find something familiar there.

"And the next one is my grandfather," Ben said. "He was a lawyer in Cleveland." A photograph of a mustached man, self-conscious and unsmiling in the manner of the day. "And *his* father, my great-grandfather." A sepia portrait from the midnineteenth century. "Our family landed on Nantucket in the 1600s."

In neighborhoods all around us, families would have completed the *yontef* meal before the customary fast and have started the walk to *shul,* leaving *yahrzeit* candles to burn on kitchen counters. Remembering their dead.

Just outside this Italian restaurant, I could picture men in their *tallises,* women with their heads covered, small boys wearing small yarmulkes, girls in dresses holding their fathers' hands—parading down the streets as I once did. In synagogues, Torahs rested in their arks, dressed in embroidered velvet and gleaming silver. When three stars appeared in the darkening sky, arks would be opened and all would rise. The Kol Nidre service would commence in all its plaintive beauty.

Landed on Nantucket in the 1600s. It made no sense, and all kinds of sense. But before I had even a moment to digest it, Michael's phone began vibrating on the table. As he picked it up, I saw that it was Jacob. He knew we had been meeting with Ben and Pilar, and surely figured lunch must be over.

I panicked.

"Go take it outside," I urged Michael. I didn't want Ben to feel pressed or railroaded.

The sense of the fragility of our bond returned full force. As Michael began to rise, Ben stopped him.

"It's okay," he said gently. "It's fine."

Michael handed me the phone. Our boy's face filled the screen.

"We're still with Ben and Pilar, honey," I said. "Do you want to say hello?"

I turned the phone's screen to Ben. He took it from me and looked at his grandson.

"Hi, Jacob—how're you doing? It's very nice to meet you."

"I'm good! It's great to meet you too!"

In the architecture of extraordinary moments that had begun the previous June—so many instances that were singular, inexplicable, beautiful, and deeply mysterious—watching a seventy-eight-year-old man meet his seventeen-year-old grandson on FaceTime felt sacred. Something loose within me settled. If nothing else happened—if we never saw one another again—Jacob and his grandfather had acknowledged each other, as if to simply say: *there you are.*

None of us wanted to part. After we made our way out of the restaurant and onto the street, we walked Ben and Pilar to their car, which was parked across from the synagogue around the corner.

"You know, Emily is interested in knowing you," Pilar said.

"I'm interested in knowing her as well," I answered.

"You should write to her," Pilar said.

"I didn't know if it was okay."

I thought of Emily's smoke signal to me via Twitter. *I see you.* And mine back to her. *I see you, too.* What would it mean to get to know my half sister?

"I'm sure I'm going to hear from her tonight, asking how our lunch went," Pilar said with a twinkle in her eye. "What do you think I should tell her?"

"Tell her it couldn't have gone better."

In our remaining moments I let Ben and Pilar know that I would be in Portland during my book tour the following spring. This seemed to be a relief to all of us—the idea that we'd be able to get together again.

"We'll come to your reading!" Ben said.

And then we hugged goodbye—each one of us hugged the others—and this time there was no awkwardness. Only a sense of having been visited by some kind of grace.

When Michael and I arrived back home later that evening, I looked through my cupboards for my usual stock of *yarhzeit* candles, but it turned out we had none. I would light no candles in memory of my complicated, beloved, dead parents on the night that I met Ben Walden. Instead, I tried to hold all of them in my overflowing heart.

Later a rabbi will remind me that the Hebrew word for father, *abba,* is composed of the first two letters in the alphabet: *aleph, bet.* He will ask me if I can accept the two tributaries—these two fathers I come from. I will learn to accept the two tributaries, in time. Their convergence is the story of my life. But on that night, I sat alone on the chaise in my office, the same chaise where less than four months earlier I had discovered the truth of my paternity, and I wrote Ben a note of thanks. I signed this one *With love.*

Part Four

42

I would have thought, in the aftermath of my lunch with Ben, that I would have felt somehow better. Relieved, perhaps. Consoled by the loveliness of the encounter. After all, it was just about the best possible outcome, for a donor-conceived person. I found myself describing it as miraculous—which I believed it was—but it was not *only* miraculous.

I was in a deeper despair that surprised me. Sensitive to bright light, startled by the most harmless noise—a clanging pipe, a slammed door would make me jump—I continued to spend most days in my house, burrowing into the history of donor insemination, reading academic papers quoting ethicists and philosophers on the rights of donor-conceived children, and further books on *halachah*, as if I might find a single key that would unlock a door leading to everything I still didn't know.

Sometimes, late at night, exhausted, emotionally spent, I would end up on websites displaying catalogs of sperm donors. I scrolled through page after page. These men used handles like Le Artist, 100 Watt Smile, McDonor, Coach of the Year, and Mission Accomplished. While on these websites, I would feel faintly uncomfortable, voyeuristic, as if I had gone to a place where I didn't belong.

If asked, I wouldn't have been able to articulate what I was looking for, why I was perusing catalogs of sperm donors. The biblical story of Joseph and his brothers came flooding back to me, along with a passage from Thomas Mann's novel of the same name.

> His desire to set a new beginning to the chain of events to which he belonged encountered the same difficulty that it always does: the fact that everybody has a father, that nothing comes first and of itself, its own cause, but that everybody is begotten and points backwards, deeper down into the depths of beginnings, the bottoms and abysses of the well of the past.

We came from different worlds, Ben and I, and we had lived different lives—unshared lives—but everyone has a father, and he was mine. He begat me—to use the ancient language—and therefore a connection existed between us so powerful it felt impossible to grasp. As I scanned the biographical information of these men, I wondered if they understood—really understood—what they were doing. I clicked on some of their profiles: all were described as handsome, and bearing similarity to celebrities ranging from Kurt Cobain to Cary Grant. And many were listed as anonymous. *Anonymous, anonymous, anonymous.* They were not willing to be contacted when the child turned eighteen. They wished to donate, and be done with it. Could a man donate sperm, check the "anonymous" box, and—emotionally speaking—be done with it? Or, as Ben had done many decades earlier, perhaps such thing could be compartmentalized.

Well over a decade earlier, Michael and I had tried to expand our own family. We hadn't wanted Jacob to be an only child. But his illness as a baby had consumed us for some years, and we had waited until we were certain he was going to be okay. By then, I was in my forties. Months of "trying" led to relatively low-tech intrauterine inseminations. Michael experienced his own version of a cubicle with its assortment of porn. I had one miscarriage, then a second one—this time at the end of my first trimester. We gripped hands in my obstetrician's office as we were told that the heartbeat was faint, then—a week later—gone. I clutched my belly and wept as the possibility that we could have a second baby of our own dwindled to nothing. Jacob was, by this point, six years old. The age difference between him and a possible sibling was growing wider with each passing month.

Nights, Michael and I sat side by side on the sofa in our library, leafing through photos and brief biographies of young women—egg donors—in an attempt to replace, or even improve upon my aging, faulty biology. We looked at Jewish donors, athletic donors, Ivy-educated donors, former model donors. We pored over handwriting, dismissing certain young women for ridiculous reasons: one dotted her *i*'s with hearts. Another had gone to an evangelical university. What did that have to do with their genes? Our obsession and confusion grew in equal measures. Without knowing it or sensing it, we slipped into the gray, murky world that my parents had once lived in; an atmosphere in which we felt shame, failure, pain, and were offered a sliver of hope. Even at the time, I thought of us as putting blinders on, eyes on the prize. I knew that if we stopped to ponder all of the possible implications of our actions, we would grind to a halt.

We did know one thing for sure, so obvious to us that we barely had need to discuss it. This baby—if there were to be a baby—would always know her origin. It would be woven into her earliest life like a bright thread, with no fanfare. We knew plenty of parents of donor-conceived kids who had beautiful families. Some had told their children, and others hadn't. I felt uncomfortable around the kids who weren't aware of their true identities. How was it possible that I knew something so fundamental about them that they didn't know themselves? How could the parents believe this was for the best? I couldn't imagine—so I told myself—going through life carrying such a secret.

But of course I had been just like those kids, and my parents like their parents. The problem, it now seemed to me, was anonymity—the promise of it, the desire for it. The hidden disaster was secrecy, the pretense and magical thinking, the certainty that no one ever needed to know. It wasn't that my parents had sought to conceive a baby in this manner—unorthodox and lawless as it once was—but that they had banished the truth even from themselves, thereby obscuring it from me. I'd begun to understand how it might have happened, still, their choices had formed my inner world as a place of cracks and fissures, lacunae of a lost child who intuited her own otherness and blamed herself for it. I understood that otherness now. I had just had lunch with it.

Secrecy and anonymity had been the prevailing wisdom fifty, sixty years ago. But now? As I opened website after website, I wondered how many children were still being born into a lie. Donors continued to stay in the shadows—or at least many of them planned to. Of course, in today's world the very idea that anonymity could be guaranteed was ludicrous, but there it was, again and again. I recalled Alan DeCherney's rueful words. *Now there are no more secrets.*

I decided to pay a visit to the California Cryobank, America's largest sperm bank. I wanted to witness the contemporary landscape of assisted reproduction, not as the frightened, clueless consumer I had been years earlier but as a person who possessed the long-secret information about her own origins.

On a classic Los Angeles late afternoon, the sky cloudless, palm trees rustling in the slightest breeze, I craned my neck skyward, staring at a six-thousand-gallon stainless-steel silo towering over a two-story building in a residential neighborhood. It was filled with vials of sperm frozen in liquid nitrogen, surrounded by barbed wire and a sophisticated alarm system. It felt as if I were staring at the future—as if encased in that silo were the eventual populations of several small countries.

Beside me was the California Cryobank's founder, Cappy Rothman, a spry eighty-year-old urologist known as the God of Sperm. Rothman had slicked-back, long white hair and piercing blue eyes. He had come on the reproductive medicine scene well after the time of my conception, so he wouldn't be likely to have information or background for me. His interest wasn't in the history I was working so hard to understand, but in the future. I was curious about the future too—struck hard by the many stories I'd read and heard from men and women who felt exiled from their own identities, set apart by a lack of information.

"How many souls—potential souls—do you have here?" I asked as I tried to take in a campus that looked like a small, well-protected nuclear arsenal. I used the term *soul* purposefully. I wanted to sort out whether Rothman thought of the lives that would be potentiated by these vials of sperm—or whether his interest stopped at the point of purchase. In the Cryobank's catalog, I had noticed that childhood photos could be purchased à la carte, along with a three-generation history, a recording of the donor speaking about his areas of interest, even examples of poetry, songs, essays, and drawings. Parents—and perhaps children—would be able to listen to the sound of a donor's voice, or read a handwritten sonnet. I wondered whether such biographical bits and pieces would ever be enough.

Rothman paused, as if he had never considered the question. There were hundreds of cylinders, and each—as I saw when we entered the interior and Rothman pried a few open for me—contained thousands upon thousands of tiny vials of sperm, bobbing in the vapor.

"Millions, I guess," he said. "Millions of souls."

It was a far cry from the small, secretive world my parents had encountered in Philadelphia in 1961. The technology to freeze sperm did not yet exist. Of course they'd had no catalog. No websites advertising dreams and possibilities, or examples of their potential donor's dream lunch date, as if this were a Proust Questionnaire. Did my parents sit in Edmond Farris's office, debating the merits of certain men? I truly didn't think so. The decorous, polite euphemisms of the day would have sufficed. Would an attempt have been made to match my dad's coloring? Would they have paid attention to blood type? Unlike many prospective parents of today—us included—my parents would not have wished for the curriculum vitae of their donor. They would have wanted to block him out, to explode him into bits and particles that left only a microscopic trace. *Leave it to us,* my parents may have been told. That is, if they were clearly told anything at all.

In Rothman's second-floor office, we sat surrounded by replicas of famous paintings. Van Gogh's *The Starry Night* was hung next to one of his self-portraits, all made up of swirls of swimming sperm. Later, Rothman will send me sperm bank swag: a ballpoint pen displaying a tiny floating plastic embryo; a T-shirt printed with a version of Edvard Munch's *The Scream* with a sperm who looked a bit like Casper the Friendly Ghost. It was difficult to tell whether his campy self-presentation was a kind of performance art, or his holy grail—or perhaps a bit of both. He had fashioned himself as a creator of life. The more life, the better.

I started to tell Rothman about my own recent discovery. It was hard to keep his attention, but eventually I did manage to stutter out the story. He looked distressed when I got to the part about finding Ben. Unsurprisingly, he and many other directors of sperm banks believe that doing away with anonymity would destroy the industry. And this may be true. If Ben had known, as a young medical student, that his identity might someday be found out, he would never have done it. I would not exist.

"What about disclosure?" I asked him. "Do you counsel parents to tell their children about their origins?"

He shrugged. "That's up to them, really. We don't get involved. I don't see what difference it makes."

"It can be very traumatic," I said. "To not know. And then to find out."

I was starting to get emotional. All those metal cylinders containing tiny vials, each vial filled with a staggering number of frozen sperm. When we had walked through the facility earlier, I had noticed shipping containers with metal canisters filled with liquid nitrogen, capped with bright yellow stickers: DO NOT RETURN EMPTY VIALS. The frozen sperm of donors like Le Artist and Coach of the Year were carefully packed into reinforced corrugated cardboard and loaded onto FedEx trucks or into the cargo holds of airplanes, heading god knows where. Millions. Millions of souls.

"Why is it traumatic?" Rothman looked puzzled. "You're here, aren't you?"

I had heard this logic before. Would I have preferred not to have been born? Of course not. I was grateful for my life. Grateful that Ben Walden had a free hour on the day of my conception. Grateful for the potent combination of my parents' courage and despair, even for their capacity to put those blinders on. But gratitude and trauma weren't mutually exclusive.

I spoke slowly. "It's traumatic because I'm fifty-four years old and I found out that the father I adored, the father who raised me, was not my biological father. That the family I thought I came from is not my biological family. That my ancestors are not my biological ancestors."

Rothman sat back in his chair and assessed me. A look of genuine compassion flitted across his face.

"I can see how that would be difficult," he said, and then he brightened. "But you look fantastic for fifty-four," he said. "You got good genes."

The intrauterine inseminations, the hormones, the catalogs of shiny young women that Michael and I had perused, the meetings with doctors, therapists, professionals, more than one cross-country trip, all took place in an increasingly frantic blur. Each step led us deeper and deeper down a rabbit hole in which the moves were choreographed to appear logical and sane. And they *were* logical for many people. But not for us. I sleepwalked through that time as if some buried part of me knew that I was in familiar territory. History on repeat. What vestiges, scraps of dialogue, exchanged glances, closed doors, harsh whispers clung to me over the years, had me feeling—as we tried for a second child, as a child became a *goal*—as if I had stepped into the rehearsal of a play whose lines I already knew by heart?

We walked away, in the end. We decided that our little family of three was exactly the right number for us—that Jacob's life as an only child would be happier than mine. It might have been different, had we had no children—had we been determined to become parents at any cost. But it was a sense I had that this path was dangerous for me. I didn't understand why. But something told me that we might just be ruining our lives. Misery, heartache, denial, secrets, grief were all tied up in it. All I knew was that I felt suffocated, paralyzed, by choices I couldn't bring myself to make, and a future I couldn't fathom.

I wasn't thinking about our own brief, frenzied foray into the realm of assisted reproduction on the day I discovered my father wasn't my father. Nor when I first recalled my mother's precise words on the Saw Mill River Parkway, followed by Susie's suggestion that I delve deeper. I at first drew no parallels between my parents' experience and my own when I realized I was donor-conceived and the tumblers all spun open and I found Ben.

It is a measure of true adulthood that we are able to imagine our parents as the people they may have been before us. My mother: not yet the full-blown narcissist borderline with the raging temper. My father: not yet the fragile man consumed by his own sorrow. But the two of them—young, vibrant, still in love with each other, wishing, hoping, praying for a life that would offer them a family, recompense for their struggles. As time went on and my shock began to dissipate, I was able to reach back into the world before me and picture them: flawed, optimistic, subscribing to the theories of the day, giving themselves over to the perceived wisdom of others.

Not long after I met Ben, I found an unopened box of my mother's buried in our basement, containing notes and cards from my birth. Among them, a telegram from a rabbi in Israel addressed to my grandparents, congratulating them on the great mitzvah of the arrival of their tenth grandchild. At the very bottom of the box was a small florist's card written to my mother in my father's hand:

> *Dearest darling,*
>   *It's been long. It's been hard. But like you always do, extra special.*
>   *All my love, Paul*

43

One day, while cleaning out my desk drawers, I found a card Susie had written to Jacob on his bar mitzvah, four years earlier. *Redeemable for the portrait of your great-grandfather Joseph Shapiro,* the card read. Susie had inherited the portrait of our grandfather when Shirley moved to Chicago. It had been a sore point for me, though I had never said so. That portrait of our grandfather had hung over the fireplace in my grandparents' apartment. In a family that prided itself on its portraits, this was the definitive portrait of the family patriarch: large, painterly, formidable. Our grandfather was stately in a dark gray three-piece suit, a hand resting on a book, his pince-nez balanced on the bridge of his nose. He looked like a man in control of his destiny. I held some sort of magical belief that being in possession of his portrait would mean I was also in control of mine.

I had wondered why Shirley had given the portrait to Susie and was secretly pleased, and surprised, that Susie planned to bequeath it to Jacob. I hoped Jacob would hang it in a future home—an heirloom, a relic of his heritage. But would the portrait still be redeemable, now that Joseph Shapiro was no longer Jacob's great-grandfather? The question was at once piercing and irrelevant. I knew Jacob would have no interest—might never have had any interest—in this long-dead man, whether or not he was related to him. Regardless, it was still stunning that part of our lives was over, sealed like a time capsule containing grainy documentary footage, a yellowed *tallis,* silver, filigreed *tallis* clips, and framed photographs of the people I had once believed were ours.

Susie had fallen away from me again with astonishing ease, in fact with something like relief. Our lifetime of disconnection, finally explained. For a brief time after my initial discovery, we had several phone conversations in which we tried to parse out what our father may or may not have known. I asked Susie if she had always suspected I wasn't our father's child. Was that why she'd brought up the practice of confused artificial insemination, all those years ago? Indeed, she had suspected, she told me.

"Why?" I asked her.

"You just looked so . . . *Christian,*" she answered.

I turned my attention to my other half sister, not the distrusting one hovering on the periphery of my childhood but the one with whom I shared a blood tie. Ben and Pilar had given me permission—something I felt I needed in order to contact her. They had been warm and forthcoming, yet with each passing day, I touched on the sense that part of me would now and forever be a wanderer. A stranger in a strange land. The language of the Torah regularly rose up from a deep place within me as if stirred from the bottom of a giant cauldron. *The Lord will scatter you among all peoples, from one end of the earth to the other end of the earth.* Exile was a theme in which I was well schooled.

Banishment and its aftermath were stitched into every biblical story I could think of. Even my Jacob's Torah portion for his own bar mitzvah had been *Bamidbar,* a dreadfully boring passage in which God asks Moses to conduct a census of the twelve tribes of Israel who wander in the desert.

I had begun to call upon friends and acquaintances—rabbis, ministers, Buddhist monks, philosophers—to ask for guidance. I knew these remarkable people because I had written a spiritual memoir when Jacob was a little boy, as a way of reconciling my beliefs—or lack of beliefs—with my religious background. I was in a spiritual crisis at the time, but now it seemed as if I must have known that someday I would need to summon an army. Now, I was in a crisis of the soul. If I didn't know how to locate myself—in the roots of my history, in the geography that had formed me—how was I supposed to make sense of the rest of my life?

A guru told me—with a certainty I couldn't help but envy—that the dead do not feel pain. When we die, she said, we survey it all: the whole complex human catastrophe we've left behind. We see patterns and designs from the great distance of death, and understand our life's purpose, after the fact. An expert in the philosophy of yoga pointed me to a book on karma. The director of a holistic institute promised me that when I got to the other side of my own searing pain, I would be set free. She suggested I stand in front of each portrait of the people I had believed to be my ancestors, and ask: *Who are you to me?*

Just before Hanukkah, I called David Ingber, a rabbi who had become a colleague and a friend. It had been six months since my wandering had commenced. After listening to my entire story, he quietly said: "You can say, 'This is impossible, terrible.' Or you can say, 'This is beautiful, wonderful.' You can imagine that you're in exile. Or you can imagine that you have more than one home."

At the end of our conversation, I wished the rabbi a Happy Hanukkah.

"Happy Hanukkah," he replied back. "And"—he laughed—"Merry Christmas!"

In the spirit of beautiful, wonderful possibilities, I wrote Emily Walden a note on her Facebook page and received an email back from her the following day. Her correspondence felt instantly familiar. How to explain it? Each of us—two women close in age, married a similar length of time, with children who were also close in age—curled up with our morning coffee once a month or so and wrote letters that grew longer with each exchange.

Here's a photo I took on my morning walk. This is the view out my window.

Both of us, shy, strong, quiet, loyal, sensitive. Both of us, serious about our work, fierce about our kids, devoted to our long-lasting female friendships. *I'm trying to be more intentional of late, to reconnect with the important people in my life. I'm home alone, a rare and savory occurrence.* I had recently taken an online version of the Myers-Briggs personality test and discovered that I am an INFJ—introverted, intuitive, feeling, judging—a category that makes up less than one percent of the population. I had a feeling that Emily might also fall into that one percent. Which of our qualities could be understood as inherited? What had formed us?

She had grown up in Portland, daughter of Ben and Pilar—a physician and his immigrant wife. She was the oldest of three.

She had gone to church with her parents every Sunday morning of her childhood. Photos of Emily showed a dark-haired, lanky, pretty little girl, a fresh-faced teenager at camp and on school field trips. Ben was right. We did look a lot alike, despite our very different coloring. On the opposite edge of the country, I had grown up the only child of Paul and Irene—an observant Jewish stockbroker and a former advertising executive turned unhappy homemaker. I had gone to synagogue with my dad every Saturday morning of my life. Similar photos existed of me: a gap-toothed, grinning girl, an awkward high school student wearing a crewneck sweater and corduroys. It was so strange, now, to contemplate our different worlds—and yet the profound, intimate genetic link of having the same father.

Just as I'd thought about Ben, I considered the many ways my path might have crossed with Emily's over the years. It seemed Emily and I might easily have friends and experiences in common. In time, we will discover that we have followed the work of the same meditation teacher, and that Emily has friends who have been to Hedgebrook, a women-only writers' retreat in the Pacific Northwest where I've taught master classes. The degrees of separation between us were few. We may have been in audiences together, at literary readings, or meditation talks. We might have attended the same parties; despite our six-year age difference, we attended graduate school at the same time. Ferries, trains, buses, planes—*millions of souls*—brushing up against one another, knowing nothing.

But then there were other ways in which Emily and I were products of our different universes. Those YouTube videos I had watched in the tense weeks waiting to hear whether Ben was willing to meet me depicted a big, boisterous family celebrating Christmas. One Saturday morning, I awoke to a long note from Emily in which she included a photograph she'd taken of a recipe card, stained brown from use.

> Alice Walden (our biological grandmother) was an amazing woman. She never went to college, as she cared for her ill mother. But she was really bright and articulate—my dad says she used to read the dictionary for fun. I've attached a recipe of hers for you.

I stared at the handwriting for a few moments, studying it. Alice Walden. Ben's mother. Emily's grandmother. *My* grandmother, technically speaking. Was it my imagination or was there something familiar in the way Alice Walden shaped her letters? Could there be anything genetic to be understood about the way handwriting evolves over generations? It seemed possible. Then I turned my attention to the recipe itself, which was for something called Twenty-four-Hour Lettuce Salad.

The instructions were to pat a broken-up head of lettuce into the bottom of a casserole dish, preferably a pretty glass one, then add celery, green onions, peppers, and water chestnuts over the lettuce, cover with an entire cup of mayonnaise, sprinkle with sugar, cheese, salad seasoning, and refrigerate for twenty-four hours, adding bacon bits just before serving.

If I had been tasked to invent the most *goyishe* recipe imaginable, I don't think I could have come up with anything to improve upon it. The cheese and bacon bits—mixing dairy with meat, bacon no less—were about as *treyf* as a meal could get, in the Yiddish idiom of my childhood. Not to mention the very idea of a salad casserole, refrigerated overnight. While the Waldens were dining on their grandmother's Twenty-four-Hour Lettuce Salad, in the home of my childhood we were eating chicken soup with matzo balls, meat-filled *kreplach,* gefilte fish topped with bright red horseradish sauce.

Emily's hymns. My *Shabbos* prayers. Her Christmas tree and tinsel and caroling. My family's silver menorah—the one I use to this day—candles blazing each Hanukkah in the bay window of my childhood home. The large, contented, peopled world in which she was raised. The small, confusing, solitary world that I escaped from. Her father—our father, yet in so many ways not my father—with his pink cheeks and thoughtful, kind demeanor. My father—the one whose voice I will hear for the rest of my life—singing the *Birkat Hamazon,* the grace after meals. If I close my eyes now, I can bring him back to me. *Shir hama-a lot beshuv Adonai, et shivat Tzion, hayinu k'cholmim. Az yimalei s'chok pinu, u'lshoneinu rinah.* His voice is off-key, plaintive, beseeching, and when our eyes meet across the dining table, he smiles at me and reaches over to pat my hand. *A song of ascents. When the Lord will return the exiles of Zion, we will have been like dreamers. Then our mouths will be filled with laughter, and our tongues with songs of joy.*

Emily and I continued our slow, long cross-country volley, increasingly sharing details of our lives. Our sons were both looking at colleges. Each of them was musical, and particularly good at math. Our kids had taken part in marches and protests in reaction against the recent presidential election. We were both consumed with and disturbed by the news. I found Emily to be enormously empathic as I shared more of my story with her, and any caution she may have felt began to fall away. We started to make a plan to get together in late spring, when I would be stopping in Portland on my book tour. *Hope and curi-*

osity was how she described her feelings toward me. Those words described how I felt as well.

One afternoon I opened an email from her that included a passage from the work of Pema Chödrön, a Buddhist teacher and writer whom I had long admired. "To be fully alive, fully human, and completely awake is to be continually thrown out of the nest. To live fully is to be always in no-man's-land."

I had felt every day since the previous June that I now lived—exiled, forever wandering—in no-man's-land. But the truth was that this had always been the case. Any thought of solid ground was nothing more than an illusion—not only for me but for all of us. Those words: *Completely awake. Live fully,* sent to me by the half sister I had never known. I had strived for those states of being all my life, while a part of me slumbered. *We will have been like dreamers.* Now there would be no more slumber. *You will be set free.*

44

As I continued to correspond with both Ben and Emily, I tried to loosen my own reins on the very notion of certainty. It was no longer a desirable state, especially since I had spent my whole life being so certain and so wrong. Instead, I tried to ride each new wave like a surfer: fluid, balanced, focused, come what may. Over the holidays, I made batches of Christmas cookies. Why Christmas cookies? It was very nearly a joke, but it was also a kind of permission. *Merry Christmas,* David Ingber had said. I liked Christmas cookies. Why couldn't I bake them? I sprinkled gingerbread men and wreaths with red and green, allowed them to harden, and placed them in a jar on our kitchen counter. We lit Hanukkah candles each night, and Jacob and I chanted the *brachot.* Genetically speaking I was half Ashkenazi Jewish, half Anglo-Saxon Presbyterian. My ancestors, scattered far and wide. There could be confusion in that—or liberation. The choice was mine.

I had been reading up on the rare hereditary eye disease Ben had told me about—the one medical condition he felt it was important for me to know. When I paid a visit to the ophthalmologist, indeed a test revealed that I exhibited early signs of the disease. It was a condition that might affect me in later years, causing light to become diffuse, occluding my night vision. The worst-case scenario would be a corneal transplant, way down the road. I learned that the recessive form is present prenatally, and certainly by the time of birth. I was not my father's child. The eyes through which I saw the world from the moment they opened were eyes that I inherited from Ben Walden.

To: Dani Shapiro
From: Ben Walden
Subject: Thanks

Hi Dani,
Thanks so much for the poem by W.S. Merwin. I'll plan to put it on my blog. It poignantly touches on the gift of aging and remembering. The other day I was visiting two residents in a nursing home and talked to a frail fellow who had recently fallen out of bed. By taking time, sitting and listening, he told me about his days as a trombone player with all the big name bands. It was fun to see him light up as the memories poured forth.

Pilar sends her warm regards to you, Michael and Jacob.

Love, Ben

This is what we had begun to do, Ben and I. We exchanged quotes. When I came across something I thought he might like, I made a mental note to pass it along to him. An essay on an Australian website about faith; a reference to Walt Whitman's "Hospital Visits" on Brain Pickings; a haunting poem forwarded to me by a friend. I wrote him about a favorite novel, Wallace Stegner's *Crossing to Safety,* and he wrote back that it was one of his favorites as well, so much so that he had recently read it for a second time. Was it a coincidence that we both loved the Stegner? Our literary sensibilities were remarkably similar. This overlap in our consciousnesses felt like a comfort and a loss, all at once. Michael described what we were doing as a grown-up version of exchanging mixtapes. A way of a biological father and daughter who had never known each other saying: this is who I am. *Thoughtus.*

At the same time as Ben and I deepened our connection—the meadows surrounding my house blanketed in a hard layer of snow, the lakes frozen, dotted with the dark shapes of ice fishermen—my dad began to reappear. He emerged in my internal world as if he had been patiently waiting for me to be ready for him. At times, I would look up from a book I was reading and see him sitting there in his favorite cabled vest, a yarmulke covering his head.

In Hebrew the word for soul is *neshama.* It is variously translated as wind, or breath. Try to capture it and it disappears. I was once again able to feel my father's presence, those unmistakable chills running the length of my body. He seemed intent on letting me know that he was there. He looked at me with the distant benevolence of the ghost he was. He gave a single, slow nod, as if to acknowledge his sorrow that he wasn't able to come back to help me—that I had to navigate this hazardous terrain alone.

I dug up some notes I had taken years earlier, during a phone session with a medium. I had never quite believed in mediums or psychics, nor did I remember any urgency at the time about contacting the dead. My literary agent had urged me to make the appointment, and I tended to do whatever she suggested. Now, I scanned the torn-out notebook pages as if they were a relic from another era. The medium and I had spoken of my parents, but this all fell into the category of *before*. Before I knew the truth—about them, about me. I almost just shoved the notes back into the file cabinet, but then I got to the part about my father. *He apologizes for not speaking the truth in your childhood. A lot left unsaid. He says someday you will understand why he needed to walk this path alone.*

The words hadn't resonated with me back then. I had been skeptical of the whole enterprise. But now they stood out. Certainly there had been a lot left unsaid. The truth hadn't been spoken. He had been solitary and had set himself apart. And now my father's apology—there in my own handwriting, as dictated by the medium—assumed an entirely new potential meaning. He was trying to tell me something. It was almost as if he knew what was in store for me.

I watched a documentary by a Canadian filmmaker named Barry Stevens, who learned as a young man that he had been donor-conceived and began searching for his biological father in midlife. Stevens interspersed research into his paternity with film footage from his childhood in which he and his parents—his mother and his social father, as it turned out— were on vacation in California. The footage shows a man trailing several feet behind his family as they walk outside a winery. His head is slightly bowed, his hands clasped behind his back. He appears nearly servile, as if he feels undeserving to be walking alongside them. It made me think of my father and his own diminishment. My mother's disgust, her patronizing tone when she spoke with him or about him, her pure and unmistakable contempt. This, too, I always had believed

I understood—and found narratives, reasons to support my understanding—but now my father's retreat from the world seems to be, at least in part, the price he paid for becoming my father.

I spent my entire adult life trying to make him proud. Not a day had passed since his death during which I didn't think of him, or silently confer with him. My initial piercing sorrow at our lack of biological connection had begun to fade, as had the double sorrow as I came to believe he'd carried the truth in his heart. Through the medium, he'd apologized to me for leaving so much unsaid. But how could he have said it? How, when the complex web of doctors and specialists insisted that silence was best for the entire family? I heard Shirley's voice once again: *Knowing what you know, you're more of a daughter to Paul than you can possibly imagine.* I may have been cut from the same cloth as Ben Walden, but I was and forever would be Paul Shapiro's daughter. Haskel Lookstein's voice joined Shirley's in my head: *Kol hakavod to your father. All the honor.* If not for him, I would never have been born. I was connected to him on the level of *neshama,* which had nothing to do with biology, and everything to do with love.

45

At a conference in Miami that winter, I attended a talk by Luke Dittrich, a journalist who had written a book about his grandfather, the surgeon famous for performing a lobotomy on a severely epileptic man which had the unintended consequence of complete and irreversible memory loss. The man became known as Patient H. M. and was, for the next sixty years, the most studied patient in the history of neuroscience. Dittrich's grandfather had been a prolific lobotomist, performing thousands of these psychosurgeries during the 1940s and '50s, a time during which the procedures were considered the last best resort for certain brain injuries and mental disorders.

Today, of course, the idea of driving a sharp instrument through the eye with a mallet in order to sever the brain's prefrontal lobe is barbaric and insane. But at the time, in the United States alone, forty thousand people were lobotomized. The surgeons performing lobotomies believed they were doing good, important, humane work. One of the surgeons who developed the lobotomy even won the Nobel Prize, though recently there has been a movement to rescind the prize, calling the innovation a massive error in judgment.

I attended Dittrich's lecture in part because I had long

been interested in the history of neuroscience but also because the subtitle of his book—*Patient H. M.: A Story of Memory, Madness, and Family Secrets*—caught my eye. His family's secrets were very different from my own, but what he and I shared was the long lens through which we were forced to see the context of the times. In the 1940s, lobotomies were normalized. People—patients, their families—were told the procedure would help. They may even have been told it was a treatment. Doctors were not to be argued with—as was true when it came to the very different matter of donor conception in the early 1960s. The eugenic benefits of donor conception were discussed confidently and with no sense of self-consciousness. The children conceived in this manner were considered to have great advantages in life; they were the genetic progeny of men of science, men of fine character, men with exemplary family histories. The children would never know the truth of their origins, and the social fathers could comfortably believe whatever they chose.

But the truth was darker and more complicated than even this. Doctors inseminated patients with their own sperm, or the sperm of whoever happened to be available. There were very few clinics or hospitals that put restrictions on the number of times a man might donate, resulting in scores of half siblings in small geographical areas. I had just heard a story from a writer friend: he had been a sperm donor a couple of decades back, when he was homeless and living out of his car, having been a drug addict and ward of the state. "I made up a whole profile," he told me. "Harvard-educated, varsity tennis player. I was very popular."

"Modern notions of informed consent did not exist," Dittrich said from the auditorium stage. What did my parents sign? Were records ever kept, or were they immediately destroyed? I had tried to reach Edmond and Augusta Farris's three children—who were now in their seventies—a number of times, but they hadn't responded to my entreaties. Their son, also named Edmond, was a singer on Carnival Cruise Lines. I knew he had received my email because he mistakenly forwarded it back to me, with a note to his sister: *Sue, what do you think?*

Shame, shame, and more shame, the present overlaid on the past, casting an angry, judgmental pall. It was impossible not to question how anyone had ever thought the practices of the day were sound and safe. I wondered what the Farris offspring now thought about what their parents had done: the two of them practicing medicine without a license in their renegade institute. What did they know? Were they proud? Disturbed? Was it devastating to them that their father had been forgotten? Or perhaps there had been mishaps, mistakes—stories that hadn't turned out quite as well as mine.

"I don't want to be a presentist," the author was saying. Presentism: the anachronistic introduction of present-day ideas and perspectives into depictions or interpretations of the past. It would be easy to fall into such thinking. I had done so from the moment I discovered the truth of my identity. Those early months were taken up first with the disbelief that my parents could have ever knowingly participated in such a deceit, and then later with anger and sorrow that they had made the choices they did—even though those choices resulted in my existence. For a long while I was able to put myself in their shoes only as *myself*, product of the late twentieth and early twenty-first centuries, with all the biological, genetic, historical, and psychological tools available to me.

But now I was coming to the awareness that my young parents-to-be had none of these tools. They possessed only their own fear, shame, despair, and desire for a child at any cost. They joined hands and went deeper into the wilderness until the only way out was through. There was no going back.

And then they pretended that it never happened. They never spoke of it again—not to each other, not to family, nor to friends. My mother—now successfully pregnant—went back to her obstetrician in his office lined with celebrity head shots. As I became heavier in her belly, so, too, did her certainty grow that I was my father's child. How could it be otherwise? My mother had always had a remarkable ability to bend reality to her will. The obstetrician most likely had known nothing—or chose to know nothing—about my parents' visits to the Farris Institute.

From the pages of Finegold's 1964 book *Artificial Insemination: In A.I. the child is never told*. It was perhaps the most painful reading I had done, its language clinical and self-satisfied. Finegold was thorough, and covered matters such as A.I. and the public, A.I. and religion, A.I. and the law. Throughout, there was a stress on anonymity. The doctor described the way legal questions of paternity might be dispensed with by referring a freshly inseminated woman to an outside obstetrician unaware of the "artificial impregnation."

> To prevent the courts from establishing that a donor was the father of the child, some gynecologists mix the husband's semen with that of the donor. Some rely on the strict secrecy involved with A.I. to deter litigation. Many doctors refer their pregnant A.I. patients to an obstetrician who is not aware of the

donor insemination. If the obstetrician knows that the husband is not the father of the newborn child, it is dishonest and illegal for him to claim the husband as the father on the birth certificate . . . A well-known and respected author on infertility insists that the "white lie" is a kindly, humane act. He wrote, "It is a violation like burning fallen leaves in the street so they will not scatter over the neighbor's lawn. It is the type of offense to which the good accomplished, completely neutralizes the infraction of a law.

On the day of my birth, my father's name was entered on my birth certificate. *Dearest darling.* Now, there would be no question he was my father. *It's been long. It's been hard.* His name was on the ultimate document of identity. A white lie, a kindly, humane act no different from burning fallen leaves in the street.

46

A principle often used in theoretical physics is Occam's razor, attributed to the fourteenth-century logician whose name it bears. The principle holds that "entities should not be multiplied unnecessarily." It was later refined by Sir Isaac Newton, who wrote in *Principia Mathematica*: "We are to admit no more causes of natural things than such as are both true and sufficient to explain their appearances."

Michael had raised the principle of Occam's razor to me early in my struggle to understand what my parents had known. He told me that a popular follow-up statement in the scientific realm is "When you have two competing theories that make the exact same predictions, the simpler one is the better." I rebelled against the notion at first—reflexively, self-protectively. Nothing about my discovery was simple, and for a long while it felt safer to weave byzantine stories about deception, cover-ups, and intrigue, since these felt closer to the shock of my experience.

But scientific method eventually became a key component in my arrival at a resting place, a narrative of sorts, distrusting of narratives as I had become, for the likeliest story. The simplest explanation for my parents' pilgrimage to the

Farris Institute was that Edmond Farris was known for his use of sperm donors. Full stop. Treatments, boosts, the thicket of euphemism aside, this was what Farris *did*. And so wherever on that slide rule of consciousness versus denial that my parents found themselves, there was knowledge. Deep knowledge. Buried knowledge. In the case of my mother, I believe, acute dissociation when it came to the truth of who I was and where I came from.

As much as the most painful parts of my discovery had to do with my father—giving me insight into his depression, his physical and psychic pain, his decline—my mother was, of course, at the center of it. Though I had spent far more time thinking about what this meant for my dad, my mother had been the engine. She was active. He was melancholy, passive. She was someone who would never have taken no for an answer. His life had been lived as if "no" had been shouted at him since the day he was born. It was my mother who would have done the research and found Edmond Farris, rogue scientist, man with a plan. It was my mother who would have made the appointment. And if there was convincing to do—if the conversation ever became detailed and honest, *conscious*—it would have been my mother who would have done the convincing.

But then I was born, and whatever sequelae there might have been to the unorthodox methods surrounding my conception vanished into the ether of magical thinking. If it wasn't thought, it wasn't so. If it wasn't spoken, it hadn't happened. Except that secrets, particularly the most deeply held ones, have a way of leaching into everything surrounding them. A psychoanalytic phrase—"unthought known"—became my instrument of illumination as I poked and prodded at my history with my parents. The psychoanalyst who coined it, Christopher Bollas, writes: "There is in each of us a fundamental split between what we think we know and what we know but may never be able to think."

"I gave you life!" my mother screamed at me whenever she was at her angriest, when I wasn't complying with her wishes or to her will. "I gave you life!" I had always found it borderline funny, but also disturbing, that my mother felt the need to underscore this bedrock parental fact. On each of my birthdays as an adult, I was meant to call her—it never occurred to me that it was usually the other way around—and thank her for having me. But here were the noxious fumes, leaking from beneath the sealed door where the truth resided.

She named me Daneile. Not Danielle. Not a plain name like Lisa or Wendy—or, come to think of it, Susie—something simple and easy to pronounce. Not a biblical name like Sarah or Rebecca. Not a family name, of which there had been some perfectly fine ones: Anna, Beatrice. In *Moses: A Human Life,* the biblical scholar Avivah Gottlieb Zornberg writes that "classically, naming a child is an opportunity for self-reflection." What had my mother made of this opportunity to name her child who was already being born into such unusual circumstances? She was proud of her originality, her ingenuity in choosing a name for me that had never been chosen before. In recent months I typed my own name into Names.org to see if perhaps there might be a hint as to its origins.

Out of 5,743,017 in the United States social security public data, the name Daneile was not present. You simply have a name that no one else in America is using. For 136 years, only your parents have thought of using your name. Hoorah! You are a unique individual.

Another trenchant line from the psychoanalyst Bollas: "We learn the grammar of our being before we grasp the rules of our language." He's speaking of infancy, of course, and the underpinnings of our psyches. The grammar of my being—the mortar into which words would eventually settle—was formed by a mother who had shoved the truth of me away from her so forcefully that all that was left was a chasm, the tender ground just after a quake. Her trembling eyes, her practiced smile, trained on me. Insisting, from minute one, that I was different, special, other, and, above all, hers.

Daneile. Pronounced *Da-neel*. It was a name that called attention to itself—that required an explanation. It stopped people. I had to spell it out for official documents, or when making travel reservations, and still, more often than not, airplane tickets would arrive for Danielle, Danelle, Danyelle, Daniele. I'd be stopped in security lines when the discrepancy was noticed. All my life—in addition to being asked how it was possible that I was Jewish—I was asked if Dani was my real name. Yes, I would say. It took too much out of me to explain. Sometimes I would add that I had never thought of myself as Daneile, not once, not even as a child. I never answered to it. But was this true? Try as I might, I couldn't ask the child I once was what she understood about herself, in the grammar of her being, before the rules of her language set in.

47

One afternoon, while sitting in my office, I glanced up at the portrait of my grandmother that hung over the chaise where Michael and I had felt the first stunning blow about my paternity. *Who are you to me?* I asked the woman in the portrait. She didn't seem ready to answer. And so I reached up and removed the heavy frame from its hook. I replaced it with a piece by the artist Debbie Millman: a large, blown-up yellow legal pad on which, in the top corner, in her own script, are the words: *This, just this. I am comfortable not knowing.* I put my grandmother off to the side, to be reckoned with at a later date. I thought of John Keats's negative capability, "when man is capable of being in uncertainties, Mysteries, doubts, without any irritable reaching after fact & reason." In this direction lay freedom, and, paradoxically, self-knowledge. By my being willing not to know thoroughly who I am and where I come from, the rigid structures surrounding my identity might begin to give way, leaving behind a sense of openness and possibility.

I was beginning to see the danger in adhering to a single narrative, hewing to a story. The peril wasn't only in getting it wrong. It was in a kind of calcification, a narrowing, a perversion of reality that hardened and stilled the spirit. Back when Rabbi Lookstein had asked me which story would ease my heart, it felt impossible to me that I could survive without knowing what had been real. But I was at the threshold of understanding what Shirley had meant about my not being an accident of history. Or rather: either all of us are accidents of history or none of us are. One sperm, one egg, one moment. An interruption—a ringing phone, a knock on the door, a flashlight through the car window—a single second one way or the other and the result would be an entirely different human being. Mine was just more complicated, an accident involving vials, syringes, contracts, and secrets.

A couple of hours after Jacob was born, my mother entered my hospital room at Mount Sinai in New York City—the very same place where she had given birth to me thirty-seven years earlier and where my birth certificate had been signed. She leaned over Jacob, who was bundled in a blanket, cradled in my arms, and examined him, her face composed, masklike.

"He looks just like a Shapiro," she finally said. "He has the Shapiro forehead. And the Shapiro chin." Was my mother perversely manipulating the moment, like the magician who appears to bend a spoon without touching it? Could she have been thinking about her own experience giving birth at this very same hospital to an infant whose father was a complete unknown? I don't think so. I think that when my mother first laid eyes on her only grandson, she believed that he was my father's grandson as well.

And when Jacob was terribly sick as a baby, stricken by a rare seizure disorder about which little was understood or known—its origins possibly hereditary—I'm convinced that my mother did not lie awake at night, wondering if the time had come to tell me the truth of my paternity. After all, if the disease that threatened Jacob was hereditary, what was there to be done? There were no records. Easy commercial DNA testing did not yet exist. There was no trail of bread crumbs to follow. I confidently told the doctors that there was no family history of seizures. Choices were made, theories posited, based on more false information.

It would have been a dreadful, perhaps unforgivable thing for my mother to have withheld information from me at the time of Jacob's illness. Even if the information may have led to further frustration or a dead end, it would have been my right—as a mother of a mortally sick infant—to know it. But, though I'll never be certain, I don't believe that's what happened. The narrative my mother clung to as if it were the only buoy in the sea was the way she had managed to get through her life. It had contributed to her becoming a miserable, alien creature, a woman who radiated rage. When the careful seams of her well-honed narrative momentarily came undone—*my daughter was conceived in Philadelphia*—she quickly stitched them up again.

During the year of Jacob's illness, as Michael and I medicated him around the clock and watched him every waking moment for signs of a flicker of motion that would indicate a seizure, my mother seemed to grow more and more furious with us. As we attempted to save our child's life, she criticized us for not properly tending to his needs. One winter night she screamed at me for not having covered his head as we carried him from the front door of her apartment building into a heated waiting car. It was the seam beginning to unravel.

. . .

The box of her papers that we found in the basement—the one in which I discovered the florist's card from my father—yielded its secrets slowly. Just as in my research on the history of donor insemination, I could take only so much before I had to pack it away. It took months to examine it all: wax envelopes filled with my baby hair, labeled *Dani's spun gold,* other small envelopes containing baby teeth. There were reams of my artwork, finger paintings of a little girl who depicted her mother as a jagged-toothed monster and herself as a small, shapeless blob. If a father appeared at all, he was a faint stick figure, off to one side. My mother had saved a letter I had written to her when I was in the third grade and had apparently received a poor grade on a math quiz. In it, I promised her that nothing like this would ever happen again, and I begged her to forgive me. But it was the way it was signed that I found most unsettling: *Yours in sorrow, Daneile.*

The truth in a thousand shards all around me. I had been certain that I had never thought of myself as Daneile, nor answered to the name. But here it was, written in my own loopy, little girl script. I had always known that I hadn't felt at ease around my mother. But I hadn't known that I had been so frightened of her. *Yours in sorrow.*

Stories ran like water through my open fingers. There was a letter written by my mother to the director of a sleepaway camp I attended when I was twelve:

Daneile may not have wet hair. I am sending her with a heated comb and she must dry her hair after swimming. I would like to prevent colds as much as possible. She thinks she's a good diver, but the back arches too much. She must be watched carefully. She is allergic to insect bites and the area rapidly swells and enlarges. Usually bites are first swabbed with ammonia. She may be given Benadryl as per her pediatrician's instructions.

The letter went on for two single-spaced, typed pages filled with bullet points, with passages underlined for emphasis. Of all the box's contents, I found it most unbearable to read. My mother was presenting me as an object—valuable, delicate, not made of the stuff of the other campers. It pained me to imagine what the camp director must have thought about the fragile, high-maintenance child being entrusted to his care.

As I neared the last of the letters and documents in the box, I came upon a letter my mother had written to me only a few months before she died of lung cancer. She was concerned about three-year-old Jacob rubbing his head and worried that he might later develop migraines, which are hereditary.

Just in case, as your father had migraines somewhat . . . and as I mentioned to you, I noticed that Jacob sometimes rubs his head after he gets up from watching his little television . . .

I read the sentence over and over again. It seemed more astonishing than my memory of my mother upon first seeing Jacob at Mount Sinai. This was something even more than a physical similarity she was imagining. This was a genetic condition, something inherited. There was no mistaking the transparent overlay, the world she created on top of the world that was.

My mother's letter to me seemed to come to a close with an unusually sentimental line, all in caps: *THANK YOU FOR MAKING ME A MOMMY AND GRANDMOM.* She was dying. She was nearing eighty, and I was nearing forty. All my life she had asked for my thanks, and now—in her own way— she was attempting to thank me.

But before the letter ended, my mother added one more passage. It was another unraveling stitch in the seam. She referenced a large manila envelope filled with cards and letters sent to my parents congratulating them on my birth, and a particular, elaborate pink card that opened like an accordion. On the first page was a couple—a husband and wife—along with a stork and a brand-new baby. The final page of the card was crowded with a note in a stranger's careful cursive, congratulating my mother on the birth of a beautiful young lady, and a request to please send a photo for all the girls in the office.

My mother must not have been able to help herself. The final words in what may have been the last letter she ever wrote to me—her parting shot—were all in lowercase and in parentheses, almost as if they didn't exist at all.

(by the way, this handwritten note from mrs. farris. I had totally forgotten about it. her husband, dr. farris, was he without whom there probably wouldn't have been thee.)

48

Three of us—Michael, our attorney, and I—sat on a bench outside a probate judge's chambers in a nondescript suburban Connecticut courthouse. The long carpeted corridor was silent and empty, lined in paneled wood. As the big clock on the wall ticked a few minutes past the appointed hour, a woman came out to let us know that the judge was running behind schedule. My attorney placed his folder on his lap, and we waited for our meeting beneath the fluorescent lights. We had brought all the paperwork, and I hoped it would be in order: birth certificate, social security card, driver's license, and an official petition to the court.

Reflexively I reached up and touched my left shoulder. It was still a bit sore. Two weeks earlier and three thousand miles away I lay on a metal table in Los Angeles, in the sun-drenched studio of the tattoo artist known as Doctor Woo. My fists had been clenched, girding myself for the pain. A friend had offered to come with me. Another had suggested that I ask Woo to use lidocaine, or numbing cream. Yet another had advised premedicating with a glass of wine. But I didn't want to be accompanied on this day, nor did I wish to be numbed. The pain, if there was to be pain, was a part of this. I wanted to feel every-thing. I was marking my body, permanently memorializing the before and after of my discovery. Doctor Woo—whose delicate designs I found on Instagram as I scrolled through thousands of artists—often incorporated compasses into many of his tat-toos. The compasses were made of lines and circles so light and thin they appeared like unspooled thread, arrows so delicate it seemed they might spin.

It was my first tattoo. That there is a prohibition against Jews getting tattoos was something I was acutely aware of, and yet that was a part of it as well. It was subversive, rebel-lious. I'm half Jewish, half something else. Why not allow that, announce that—*be* that? I'm a hybrid, made of two sets of ancestors who would never have crossed paths or sprung from the same village. I had decided on my shoulder—not a hidden place, a secret spot that only those most intimate with me would see. My shoulder was visible, if I wished it to be.

The following afternoon, I had an appointment with Rabbi David Wolpe, the Senior Rabbi of Sinai Temple in Los Angeles. I had long admired Wolpe for his brilliant and incisive thinking. I had already planned to wear a cardigan, to keep my transgression private. I was afraid he would judge me—though I needn't have been concerned. I would quickly come to real-ize that David Wolpe had no time to waste on antiquated pro-priety. "We all feel as if we're other," he told me. "Any thinking person knows we *are* other. Only you've actually been to the front lines of otherness. And you've come back with something to teach us." As we sat in his quiet inner sanctum, he recited the words of Elizabeth Barrett Browning: "God answers sharp and sudden on some prayers, / And thrusts the thing we have prayed for in our face, A gauntlet with a gift in it."

In that instant—my fresh tattoo hidden beneath my summer cardigan—I understood what the rabbi was offering. My newfound awareness was both gauntlet and gift. The choice wasn't to see it as one or the other. It was to embrace it as both.

In Doctor Woo's studio—a far cry from the hallowed halls of Sinai Temple—I explained my reason for wanting a tattoo to the artist. "Last spring I found out that my father was not my biological father," I told him, keeping the story as brief as possible.

I wondered how many stories he heard every day—reasons people have for turning their bodies into canvases, vessels, statements of identity. The young donor-conceived people Wendy Kramer had told me about had desperately, fruitlessly searched for their biological fathers, until they settled for a series of numbers—the donor ID—inked into their arms as if to say: this is all I know of who I am.

"I'd like a bird," I told Woo.

"What kind of bird?" he asked.

His Instagram feed was full of birds: eagles, ravens, hawks.

"I don't want an angry bird," I said.

Woo began to sketch on a piece of paper.

"Not a fierce bird," I went on. "And not a hummingbird."

Michael had pointed out to me that hummingbirds hover. I wanted one that soared.

"Maybe a swallow," he said.

"Maybe. A sweet bird." My eyes stung. "A free bird."

On the table, as Doctor Woo began needling the bird into the front of my shoulder, I hardly felt a thing. It was as if I were floating, suspended somewhere in the in-between. My clenched fists loosened. The meditation teacher Jack Kornfield often begins his meditations by saying, "Take your seat beneath the tree of enlightenment, halfway between heaven and earth." I felt as if I were taking my seat, taking my place as a human being who had undergone a profound experience and was now integrating it, creating a sign on my own body.

Uk'shartam l'ot al yadecha v'hayu l'totafot bein einecha. I heard the words of the central prayer *V'ahavta* as if they were being chanted beside me. *Take to heart these instructions with which I charge you on this day. Impress them upon your children . . . Bind them as a sign on your hand and let them serve as a symbol on your forehead.* I had been raised with the powerful idea that we must show the world who and what we are. We must keep *mezuzot* on our doorposts, and men must wear yarmulkes on their heads. I closed my eyes as Doctor Woo continued to make me my own sign, incorporating tiny compasses, and two faint circles—hints of direction—around the swallow's beak.

Migratory birds have internalized compasses; they use earth's geomagnetic field—along with light, stars, and other cues—to guide them as they fly. I hadn't known north from south, east from west. I had been clueless about my own coordinates. Beneath all the comments I had fielded thrummed the most fundamental questions: *Who are you? What are you?* They were beneath Mrs. Kushner's baffling statement, beneath Mark Strand's icy renunciation of who I thought myself to be. It was the subtext of every pronouncement about my ethnicity. For the rest of my life, I wanted a visual reminder that now I had my own internalized compass. I knew what and who I was. Now, the map was mine.

· · ·

The judge at the Probate Court of the State of Connecticut was finally ready to see us. We all sat around a conference table, and my attorney distributed his prepared documents. The judge, wearing a suit, asked me to raise my hand and recite an oath. Then he asked why I had petitioned the court to change my given name.

"Because I hate it," I said. "Because no one can pronounce it or spell it. Because I've never answered to it." Which wasn't entirely true, of course. I had painful proof that I once had answered to it.

I signed the papers in front of the judge, county clerk, my attorney, and Michael. The document was then stamped with an official seal. An undoing. The little girl with the unpronounceable name who stared and stared at her face in the mirror, trying to understand what she was seeing, was finally a grown woman who knew who she was and where she came from. Daneile was the name that had been handed me along with so many other mysteries of my existence. But I didn't have to be stuck with it. This was something I could let go.

"Your name is now legally Dani Shapiro," said the judge.

"Just like that?" I asked.

Somehow I thought it would take longer to unravel something that had identified me for a lifetime. I hadn't understood that at that very moment, my given name would fall away, fly off like the swallow on my shoulder. Two weeks earlier I had reclaimed my body. Now I was reclaiming my name. Later, I will change all of my documents of identification save one. My birth certificate will remain the same. *Daneile, daughter of Paul.* In Hebrew that would be *Daniela bat Pinchas.* That piece of history, more true than not, can never be altered.

49

The month of May had seemed so far in the future when we'd had lunch with Ben and Pilar in New Jersey back in October, but now it had arrived and along with it, my book tour. It had been nearly a year since I'd received my DNA results. Nearly a year of living in a new reality and adjusting to it the way the body acclimates to a new temperature. There was something to the old adage that time heals all wounds. I'm not so sure about the healing, but time certainly had brought me to a place of greater acceptance that this was indeed my life. I had changed my name and gotten a tattoo. Outward signs of inward shifts. The phrase *donor-conceived* no longer traumatized me. I could look at childhood photographs of myself with my parents with curiosity as well as some measure of sorrow that I imagined would always be there—but the tremulous, mute, childlike denial of what I was seeing was gone.

Once in a while, though, while driving down a country road, or as I crossed a busy intersection in the city on my way to an appointment, or even while sitting quietly in meditation, I would be overcome by the now-familiar physical sensation of slipping into a void. I had come to understand this as the space between my father and Ben. Neither of my two fathers could ever be entirely mine. *Everyone is begotten and points backwards, deeper down into the depths of beginnings.* There was, and always would be, a groundlessness to the depths of my beginnings. That knowledge now existed in the place within me where all the secrets had once been stored and despite the occasional free-falls, felt like a new form of strength.

Which was a good thing, because in order to spend the next six weeks on the road, I had to split myself in two, take everything about the last year and shelve it. I would be promoting my latest book, which concerned itself with marriage and memory. Innumerable times, I had listed among the strange twists and turns for which I was grateful, the timing of my discovery. If I had found out the truth of my family history while I was writing *Hourglass*, it would have been a wrecking ball aimed straight at my delicate little book. The manuscript would have wound up in a drawer.

Portland. The city stood out on my calendar amid all the other tour stops. It was part of a West Coast leg that included L.A., San Francisco, and Seattle. I had been in touch with the Walden family a month in advance, and the entire day in Portland was now planned. Lunch with Ben and Pilar before my reading at Powell's Books; dinner afterward with Emily and her husband, Scott. Even Emily's older kid, Nick, was planning to come to the reading. It was nearly the whole Walden *mishpacha*. Michael was flying west to meet me in Portland. I had told him he didn't have to, that I'd be okay. "I know you'll be okay," he'd said. "But you need a witness."

To several degrees less than I'd felt the year before, when I went through the motions of my everyday life on that trip to San Francisco—making dinner reservations, calling Ubers, conferring on book jackets while attempting to metabolize the elephant—my time on tour once again had the strange quality of being on one side of a split screen while I held the rest at bay. It was hard work, this compartmentalization, this pushing away of what most consumed me. The sheer psychic effort of it was exhausting. I wondered how my parents had done it; jettisoned their knowledge of my origins. At pediatrician appointments, how had my mother given my medical history without being gripped by persistent distress? How was it that they laughed about the Kodak holiday poster, holding up their daughter as an emblem of Christmas cheer? How deep did their denial have to go—and at what cost—in order to pulverize the truth, until it no longer had shape or form?

I tried not to concern myself with these questions as I zigzagged the country. Though in quiet moments—alone, on flights, or in solitary hotel rooms—it all reemerged the way suppressed thoughts tend to do. I had been high up in the air for weeks, nearly every day, looking down at the flat plains, the mountain ranges, the world below, and it wasn't a far leap from there to think about geography and displacement. *The country I'm from*—the way I'd come to think of Ben. I had been living for a year in the lashed sea's landlessness.

I often wondered what would have been the case if my parents had made a different choice—a more radical choice for the place and time in which they lived—and had told me the truth from a young age. What if I had been raised knowing that my father and I weren't related? What if I had always known that the reason I looked different, and felt different, was in fact because I *was* different? It would be easy to fantasize that this would have been better. But we can never know what lies at the end of the path not taken. Other difficulties, other heartaches, other complexities would certainly have emerged. But at least we would have been a family traversing them together.

Michael was waiting for me when I got off the plane in Portland. We had just enough time to drop our bags off at the hotel and meet Ben and Pilar at a nearby restaurant. It was a gray, rainy day, traffic sluggish along Southwest Fifth Avenue. This time, I felt no nervousness. Only pleasure in continuing the conversation that had begun haltingly a year before and had grown into something comfortable, no matter how unusual or, at moments, disconcerting. I still had questions for Ben, ones I wasn't sure I could ask. I wanted to know more about how many times he had donated. A dozen? Fifty? If I knew what his reference to "a period of time" meant, I would have some way of imagining how many half-siblings I might have in the world.

I wasn't sure Ben wanted to think about that. And I was certain that Pilar did not. The four of us met at a steak house on the thirtieth floor of an office building, with floor-to-ceiling windows that overlooked the city and the distant, foggy outline of the Cascade Mountains. It was an airy, elegant place I sensed they'd arrived at with some care. This time, we all ordered a glass of wine, and the mood was more celebratory than cautious. Like children playing a game of tag, we knew which subjects were home base. We spoke about my tour, Michael's new film, and then about the endlessly absorbing topic of the current administration. They caught us up on their kids and grandkids, and asked after Jacob, who was finishing up his junior year. The evening's plans, carefully calibrated, meant that Ben and Pilar were coming to Powell's to hear me read, and then they were taking their grandson Nick back home with them to spend the night so that Emily and Scott, and Michael and I could go out to a late dinner.

I kept thinking about what it would be like to be in front of a crowd, speaking about my new book to an audience that included my biological father and half sister. My dad had died before I became a writer. He'd never read my work nor seen me in the context of my professional world as an author. In the thirty years since his death, I had written nine books. I had read from those books to hundreds of audiences all over the world. More times than I can count—with each new publication, or upon receiving a particularly meaningful review—I would talk to him. *Dad, look—I wrote all these books for you.*

Now my other father, my biological father, would be the one sitting in the audience watching me. Ben had written to me after our first meeting that although he could only claim a paternal genetic link, he was certainly proud of what I had accomplished, not just in my career but also in establishing a wonderful, loving family. As grateful as I was for my relationship with Ben, my heart ached for my father. He had never experienced that parental pride, that *kvelling*—the Yiddish word he would have used. Ben was now a part of my adult life. He had met Jacob over FaceTime. He had traded stories with Michael. He would stand in line to have his book signed later that evening. If my parents had been able to flash forward for just half a second to a future in which—with both of them gone—I would be dining high above the city of Portland with the anonymous medical student they had pretended didn't exist, would they have proceeded?

·   ·   ·

I would have loved to explore many of these intricacies with Ben—to ask the provocative, deep, hard questions about this strange terrain—and my sense was that he would have welcomed a complex conversation. But Pilar, despite her warmth, still seemed to be in some state of disturbance at the idea that she had never known Ben's history as a sperm donor and the fact that the three adults they had raised together were not his only children. And I could hardly blame her. I couldn't imagine how I'd feel if a child of Michael's appeared one day, upending the size and shape of our family.

As we lingered over coffee, Pilar asked a question I could tell had been haunting her.

"So you've taken your name down?"

At first I didn't know what she meant.

"From the website? From Ancestry.com?"

I was afraid to look at Michael. I wasn't sure how to answer. No, we hadn't taken my name down from Ancestry.com. In fact, we had spread my information as widely as possible among other sites—23andMe, MyHeritage, GEDmatch—to increase the possibility that I would discover half-siblings and they would discover me.

I couldn't bring myself to tell Pilar that my DNA was readily discoverable. Nor did I want to lie to her. As I was trying to formulate a response, Michael chimed in.

"Adam Thomas's DNA is still up there too," he said mildly.

"But he told us it was private," Pilar said.

Ben looked back and forth between us.

I could tell that Michael and I were having the same thought. *Let it go*. Adam Thomas's DNA was every bit as discoverable as mine. If the Waldens had asked him to take it down, he hadn't complied. Which meant that if biological offspring of Ben's found themselves on Ancestry.com, they would come up with the same mystery first cousin that I had, and—with a little ingenuity and journalistic chops—follow the trail of bread crumbs all the way to Ben.

Pilar seemed momentarily appeased by this false notion of privacy—both Adam Thomas's and my own. But then, a few minutes later, as Ben and Michael were engrossed in a different conversation, she leaned toward me and spoke with a hushed intensity.

"Your daddy is a good daddy," she said. I thought I had misheard her. She rested a hand on my arm. "He's a very good daddy," she repeated.

"Our home is your home," she went on. "You can stay with us, anytime."

I knew it had taken a lot for Pilar to let me in. But after the careful terminology—the genetic link, the biology, the delicate dance—the word *daddy* felt out of place.

"If any others come," she said, "you won't tell them. You'll stay private." It was half-question, half-statement. And suddenly I understood. How old was too old for a surprise? A young medical student's casual decision now had the potential to shake up a retired doctor's life. Surely Ben and Pilar, too, had read stories about donor-conceived people who had discovered scores of half-siblings. Had they imagined a line of blond, pink-cheeked offspring circling the block outside their home? Of course there had to be a kernel of fear, even in their interaction with me.

I laughed, as if there was something whimsical about the whole idea, and took a big sip of my abandoned glass of wine. In a way, Pilar's words provoked a train of thought I'd never before entertained: Ben as Daddy. I pictured myself sprawled on the floor in Ben and Pilar's comfortable home in their retirement community, playing backgammon. I imagined being in my pajamas and robe, drinking coffee early in the morning, reading the paper with Ben. Perhaps we'd do the crossword together. And then, like a needle scratching across a vinyl record, the thoughts screeched to a stop.

Ben was a lovely, caring man for whom I felt great fondness and gratitude. Knowing him was allowing me to put pieces of myself together in a way that would be of comfort to me for the rest of my life. He was my cloth, my country. But he was not my daddy. I felt for Pilar, I really did. She had raised a loving, tight-knit family. I resembled her husband more than any of their own children did. I'd seen a photo of Ben as a teenager, and Jacob looked a lot like him. What if, as I strongly suspected, there were others? More women or men in their early- or mid-fifties scattered around the country who were biological children of Ben's?

Here was a massive ethical conundrum, one I would explore if the need ever presented itself. Part of me hoped it would never arise, at least not in their lifetimes. The question of what I owed them—my promise of privacy—and what I owed anyone who might someday contact me, was never far from my mind. If someone like me, stunned, traumatized, shocked, disbelieving, contacted me through one of the testing sites asking how it was possible that we were listed as half-siblings, I couldn't turn that person away. I *was* that person.

At the same time, I was acutely aware of Ben's kindness in being truthful with me from the beginning, as well as his courage and generosity in ultimately wishing to meet me. My words during our first lunch: you didn't have to do this. He could have ignored me, or lied. He could have been rejecting, even cruel. Instead, Ben's inherent goodness also made me feel I came from that goodness. I felt enormously protective of both Ben and Pilar and would never want to hurt either of them.

The exchange with Pilar happened in its own cocoon, so as the four of us left the table, there was no awkwardness. She hadn't exactly asked a question, nor had I attempted to answer. Ben had no idea the conversation had even taken place. I filed it away to be considered at another time. In the following months, as a steady stream of second and third cousins on the Walden side began to appear on my Ancestry page—distant biological relatives with whom I saw no reason to connect—I'd think about the odds that a half-sibling would show up one day. And then another. And another. Who would these people be to me? And I to them? I had certainly benefitted from being the first of Ben's offspring to stumble upon the truth. If I had not been the first, would he have ever responded to me? I was lucky. I understood that now. *Recompense.* I came from two men—my dad and Ben—who were honorable to the core. *You can say this is beautiful, wonderful.* What would I do with my good fortune?

50

Later that evening I stand behind the lectern at Powell's Books, reading to a standing-room-only crowd, but I am constantly aware of the family taking up the entire fourth row. That line of warm, encouraging people is like a distant land seen from the churning sea. I take in only flashes: white hair, a blue shirt, a tall, angular man arriving late, my half sister's wide, generous smile. But even as I bracket the air in front of me, moving my small hands in the same gesture as the man I come from, there is another man—the one who loved me into being—who I am looking for. There has rarely been an event of importance in my life when I have not searched for my father. Rarely a time during which I have not felt both his presence and his absence. I silently call to him, a Hebrew word—*hineni*. Here I am. *Hineni,* uttered only eight times in the entire Torah, is less a statement of personal geography than an expression of presence and pure attentiveness. Abraham said it to God when he was asked to bind Isaac, and repeated it in response to his son. Jacob said it when he answered the call of an angel. Joseph said it to Jacob when he was sent to seek his brothers. Moses found his voice and said it to God at the burning bush. And I say it to my father, again and again. *Hineni.* I am here. All of me.

Acknowledgments

This is a story that was written as I lived it. Events unfolded in ways that were destabilizing and miraculous in equal measure. I am grateful to those who offered support.

I will begin with the family I call Walden. Your humanity and grace enabled me to move forward, to fill in the missing pieces. I will forever know just how blessed I am that you are who you are. Thank you for trusting me.

Early readers who made valuable contributions to this book are Abigail Pogrebin, Elissa Altman, Karen Shepard, and Andy McNicol.

Jennifer Mendelsohn, Wendy Kramer, Naomi Cahn, Jacqueline Mroz, Dr. Leonard Hayflick, Dr. Alan DeCherney, Dr. Jenna Slutsky Bass, Arthur L. Caplan, Daniel Wikler, Rabbi David Wolpe, Rabbi Haskell Lookstein, Sylvia Boorstein, David Crean, Jack Gilpin, Rabbi David Ingber, Elizabeth Lesser, Dr. Bessel van der Kolk, Gabrielle Bernstein, Stephen Cope, Kris Carr, you are all my heroes. Experts, ethicists, authors, doctors, spiritual leaders who took the time out of your busy lives to help me enter hidden realms.

Thanks to my research assistant, Erica Schwiegershausen, who left no stone unturned.

ACKNOWLEDGMENTS

Jennifer Rudolph Walsh, I will always treasure your guidance, friendship, wisdom, and support.

Dr. Arietta Slade helped me to navigate the unthought known.

Deepest gratitude to my beloved aunt, Shirley Feuerstein, weaver's daughter, who stitched me back together again, and again, and again.

Jordan Pavlin and the entire Knopf family, every day I pinch myself. Julie Barer, your spirit and enthusiasm are contagious. I feel lucky to have such an amazing team behind me.

And finally, my two greatest loves: Michael Maren has lived this story with me every second of the way, has read each page of this book with devotion and discernment. I don't think I could have survived this without you. And Jacob Maren, this is your story too. It—and you—couldn't be more beautiful.

A NOTE ABOUT THE AUTHOR

Dani Shapiro is the author of the memoirs *Hourglass, Still Writing, Devotion,* and *Slow Motion,* and five novels, including *Black & White* and *Family History*. Shapiro's short fiction, essays, and journalistic pieces have appeared in *The New Yorker, Granta, Tin House, One Story, Elle, Vogue, The New York Times Book Review,* the op-ed pages of *The New York Times,* and many other publications. She has taught in the writing programs at Columbia, New York University, the New School, and Wesleyan University; she is cofounder of the Sirenland Writers Conference in Positano, Italy. She lives with her family in Litchfield County, Connecticut.

A NOTE ON THE TYPE

This book was set in Hoefler Text, a family of fonts designed by Jonathan Hoefler, who was born in 1970. First designed in 1991, Hoefler Text was intended as an advancement on existing desktop computer typography, including as it does an exponentially larger number of glyphs than previous fonts. In form, Hoefler Text looks to the old-style fonts of the seventeenth century, but it is wholly of its time, employing a precision and sophistication available only to the late twentieth century.

Composed by North Market Street Graphics,
Lancaster, Pennsylvania

Printed and bound by Berryville Graphics,
Berryville, Virginia

Designed by Soonyoung Kwon